The Architecture of Avoidance - How Organizations Invent Roles to Escape the Change They Need.

ISBN: 979-8-9971013-0-5

Printed in the United States of America.

For my children, who watched me rebuild myself.

For my parents, who taught me what strength looks like.

And for the professor who rewired the way I write and set me on the path to this book.

Contents

CHAPTER 1

The Room / The Question / The Silence

The meeting was scheduled for an hour. Everyone knew it would run long. The agenda was short, but the architecture beneath it was not.
The board wanted answers.
The CEO wanted cover.
The PMO director wanted survival.
The consultants wanted the narrative to hold.
And the system—silent, unrepresented, undefeated—waited for the moment it always wins.

The CEO opened with the performance of confidence.
"The transformation is on track," he said, though the milestones had slipped.
He spoke in abstractions, the way leaders do when the truth is structurally inconvenient.

The PMO director followed. Dependencies unresolved. Decision rights unclear. Priorities shifting weekly.
He tried to soften the edges without contradicting the CEO.
The consultants nodded sympathetically, the way consultants do when they recognize a pattern they have no incentive to interrupt.
The board listened, concerned but unsurprised.

Then the question surfaced, the one that always arrives, the one that cuts through narrative and lands directly on the architecture.

"Who owns this?"

The room fell into the quiet that isn't contemplation but recognition.
The PMO director looked at the CEO.

The CEO looked at the consultants.
The consultants looked at the PMO director.

No one owned it.
No one could.

Responsibility had been assigned to a role.
Authority had been retained by the structure.
The outcome was predetermined long before the meeting began.

This is where the story of the modern enterprise begins: with a substitution so subtle organizations mistook it for leadership.

The substitution of architecture with roles.
The substitution of decisions with titles.
The substitution of responsibility with symbolism.
The substitution of clarity with language.

This is the original sin.
And it always reveals itself first in the silence.

The Birth of the Substitution

The substitution didn't begin with malice.
It began with pressure.
Markets accelerated.
Technology reshaped the landscape.
Complexity outpaced the hierarchy.
Leaders felt the strain in every review, every escalation, every analyst call.
They knew the system needed to change.
But architectural change is slow, costly, and politically dangerous.
It redraws power.
It alters incentives.
It exposes the limits of the hierarchy.

Most leaders aren't rewarded for that kind of courage.
Most boards don't ask for it.
Most organizations aren't built to survive it.

So they reached for something easier.

A role.

A role could be created in a quarter.
A role could be announced in a town hall.
A role could absorb the anxiety of change without requiring the organization to change.

It looked like progress.
It felt like leadership.
It was neither.

The first substitution happened quietly.
A project manager added to a team.
A PMO created to "drive alignment."
A new title introduced to "own transformation."
Each move felt responsible.
Each move felt proactive.
Each move avoided the architecture.

The organization didn't recognize the cost.
Not yet.

But the system did.

The Lineage of Roles

The first generation appeared in the 1990s, when work began crossing functional boundaries the hierarchy couldn't support. The enterprise expanded horizontally. The architecture stayed vertical. Something had to absorb the overflow.

Project managers were introduced to coordinate work no one owned.
They were asked to "drive alignment" across functions with no incentive to align.
They were asked to "manage dependencies" created by decisions made far above their pay grade.
They were asked to "ensure delivery" without the authority to make a single structural call.

PMOs followed.
They were expected to enforce standards without the power to alter incentives.
They were expected to create clarity in environments where ambiguity was a feature, not a flaw.
They were expected to deliver predictability in systems designed for local optimization.

They were the first sacrificial roles.
They were the first to inherit fictional clarity.
They were the first to fail for reasons that had nothing to do with competence and everything to do with architecture.

The pattern expanded in the 2000s.
The Chief Digital Officer was asked to modernize systems it didn't own.
The Chief Innovation Officer was asked to challenge a structure it couldn't alter.
The Chief Transformation Officer was asked to lead change that required decisions only the CEO could make.

Each role inherited the same structural impossibility.
Each role was celebrated at creation and isolated at execution.
Each role collapsed under expectations it was never positioned to meet.

Around them, the ecosystem flourished.
Consultants discovered that a new role created a new buyer.
Associations discovered that a new role created a new credential.
Analysts discovered that a new role created a new category.
Vendors discovered that a new role created a new budget line.

The role became the product.
The definition became optional.
The ambiguity became the engine of demand.

Inside the enterprise, the consequences were predictable.
The role entered without authority, without decision rights, without structural ownership.
It entered with responsibility but no power.
It entered with expectations but no leverage.

When it failed, the failure was personalized.
The architecture escaped scrutiny.
A new role was created.
The cycle repeated.

This is the lineage of fictional clarity.
A genealogy of roles created to carry the burden of change without the power to enact it.

The Structural Proof

Across industries, the pattern is identical.
Different sectors.
Different missions.
Same architecture.
Same refusal.

A hospital system hired a Chief Innovation Officer to modernize care delivery.
She proposed new workflows, new staffing models, new digital pathways.
Every idea collided with reimbursement structures she could not change.
The architecture pulled the organization backward.

A global bank hired a Chief Digital Officer to accelerate transformation.
He built roadmaps, launched pilots, redesigned customer journeys.
Every decision ran through risk governance.
The architecture slowed every move.

A manufacturing company empowered its PMO to deliver enterprise coherence.
The PMO built standards, templates, dashboards.
Every plant optimized for its own metrics.
The architecture rewarded fragmentation.

A tech company hired a Chief AI Officer to “drive AI strategy.”
She built models, frameworks, governance.
Engineering retained all architectural authority.
The architecture determined the roadmap.

Different sectors.
Same architecture.
Same outcome.

When responsibility is assigned to a role but authority remains in the structure, the role will fail.

This is not a metaphor.
It is not a theory.
It is a law of organizational physics.

The architecture always wins because it is the set of constraints that determines what the system can and cannot do. As long as those constraints remain unchanged, the outcomes are inevitable.

Roles come and go.
Titles rise and fall.
Mandates expand and collapse.
But the architecture remains.

And because the architecture remains, the outcomes remain.

The Failure Sequence

The sequence begins long before the role is posted.

A role is created to carry the burden of change.
The announcement is framed as progress.
The architecture remains untouched.
The role inherits responsibility without authority.
The role struggles.
The struggle is personalized.
A new role is created.
The cycle repeats.

Inside one enterprise, the sequence played out in a single year.

A Chief Transformation Officer was hired with great fanfare.
She was told she would "own the transformation."
She asked for decision rights.
She was told to "influence."
She asked for structural authority.
She was told to "collaborate."
She asked for clarity.
She was given language.

She built a plan.
The architecture ignored it.
She escalated decisions.
The hierarchy absorbed them.
She pushed for alignment.
Functions optimized locally.
She tried to accelerate.
The system slowed her down.

When the transformation stalled, the narrative shifted.
She was "not strategic enough."
She was "not influential enough."
She was "not driving alignment."

The architecture remained invisible.
The failure was personalized.
A new role was created.
The cycle continued.

This is not incompetence.
This is architecture reproducing itself.

The Understory

Beneath the pattern lies the understory, the quiet truths no strategy deck names.

Leaders avoid architectural decisions because architectural decisions redistribute power.
Teams avoid structural clarity because ambiguity protects them.
Boards avoid confronting the architecture because it implicates their oversight.
Consultants avoid challenging the architecture because ambiguity is profitable.
The ecosystem avoids structural honesty because fictional clarity sustains it.

Decision rights remain with the hierarchy.
Responsibility is assigned to a role.
Incentives reinforce the status quo.
Power flows through historical channels.
Accountability diffuses.
Expectations accumulate.
Failure is personalized.
Architecture remains untouched.

If you have ever been asked to deliver outcomes without authority, you have lived inside this architecture.
If you have ever watched a role collapse and blamed the person, you have participated in fictional clarity.
If you have ever created a title to signal progress, you have contributed to the original sin.
If you have ever inherited a mandate that exceeded your position in the hierarchy, you have carried the burden of avoidance.

This chapter ends where the next begins.

Fictional clarity did not emerge from confusion.
It emerged from convenience.
It emerged from the desire to name the work without owning it.
It emerged from the belief that language could substitute for architecture.
It emerged from the institutions that monetized ambiguity.
It emerged from a system that preferred symbolic action to structural change.

To understand the lineage of failed roles, we must understand how fictional clarity became the operating language of the modern enterprise that protected the organization from confronting the inconvenient truth.

That is the work of Chapter 2.

What began as the substitution of architecture with roles quickly evolved into something more subtle and more dangerous: the substitution of architecture with language. The system learned that vocabulary could protect it from the decisions it refused to make.

CHAPTER 2

The Moment the Language Breaks Free

The leadership team gathered for what was supposed to be a routine strategy review.
The slides were polished.
The vocabulary was impressive.
The architecture was strained.
No one said that part aloud.

The COO walked through a deck filled with words that sounded decisive: "alignment," "acceleration," "modernization," "integration."
The room nodded along, relieved by the familiarity of the language.
No one asked what any of it meant.
No one wanted to reveal how little they understood.

A director raised a question about a dependency that had stalled for months.
The COO responded with a phrase that had become a shield: "We're driving clarity."
The director nodded, though nothing had been clarified.

The CTO added a new term to the conversation, "digital orchestration."
It landed with the weight of authority.
No one asked what it meant.
The room absorbed it, grateful for a phrase that sounded like progress.

The transformation lead watched the exchange.
She had seen this before.
The language was moving faster than the work.
Vocabulary was outrunning capability.
Titles were outrunning architecture.

The CEO closed the meeting with confidence.
"We're aligned," he said.

They weren't.
They were synchronized only in their relief.

This is how fictional clarity begins.
Not with deception.
With the quiet comfort of words that protect the organization from the truth.

The Origin of Fictional Clarity

The first moment of fictional clarity rarely looks like a decision.
It looks like a leader naming work they do not understand.

A VP of Operations once stood in front of her team, overwhelmed by a backlog of cross-functional issues she couldn't untangle.
She didn't know how to redesign the system.
She didn't know how to change the incentives.
She didn't know how to alter the decision rights.
So she reached for something she could control.

"We need a Program Lead," she said.

The room relaxed.
A title had been created.
The anxiety had somewhere to go.

The Program Lead arrived two weeks later.
He asked for clarity.
He was given vocabulary.
He asked for authority.
He was given expectations.
He asked for decision rights.
He was told to "influence."

The VP felt relieved.
The team felt supported.
The system remained untouched.

This is the origin of fictional clarity.
Not a strategy.
A reflex.

A title becomes a placeholder for decisions that have not been made.
A role becomes a container for ambiguity the architecture refuses to resolve.
Language becomes a substitute for understanding.

The organization doesn't drift into fictional clarity.
It reaches for it.

Because naming the work is easier than owning it.
Because appearing aligned is easier than becoming aligned.
Because speaking transformation is easier than performing it.

The Institutionalization of Fictional Clarity

Fictional clarity did not remain inside the enterprise for long.
The institutions surrounding the enterprise recognized its value before the enterprise understood what it had created.

Inside a consulting firm, a partner reviewed a slide that introduced a new role, "Head of Digital Enablement."
The title didn't exist in the client's organization.
It didn't matter.
The partner circled it with a marker.

"This will sell," he said.

The team nodded.
A role without definition is a role that requires support.
A role without boundaries is a role that requires frameworks.
A role without authority is a role that requires guidance.

Clarity was not the product.
Ambiguity was.

Across town, a professional association convened a committee to design a new certification.
They debated the curriculum for a role no one could define.
The chair finally said, "It just needs to sound like something a serious organization would have."

The room agreed.
The credential legitimized the role.
The role justified the credential.

At an analyst firm, a researcher drafted a maturity model for a role that had existed for less than a year.
The model implied a linear progression from confusion to competence.
It didn't matter that the architecture made such progression impossible.
The model created a category.
The category created demand.

Fictional clarity became institutionalized.
It became a product.
It became a marketplace.
It became an industry.

And the architecture remained untouched.

The Commercial Engine Behind Fictional Clarity

The commercialization of fictional clarity did not begin with frameworks.
It began with demand signals.

A consulting firm's leadership team reviewed quarterly numbers.
A partner pointed to a spike in inquiries for a new title, "Chief Digital Acceleration Officer."

"Is this real?" someone asked.

"It doesn't matter," the partner said. "It's happening."

The firm built a supply chain around the signal.

White papers seeded the vocabulary.
Keynotes amplified the urgency.
Benchmarks created the fear of falling behind.
Diagnostic tools converted fear into budget.

By the time organizations realized they had a gap, the market had already built the product to fill it.

This was not support.
This was production.

Roles became SKUs.
Mandates became market segments.
Anxieties became revenue forecasts.

A role that lacked definition created demand for interpretation.
A role that lacked boundaries created demand for operating models.
A role that lacked authority created demand for

escalation pathways.
A role that lacked ownership created demand for governance overlays.

The market did not need the role to succeed.
It needed the role to exist.

Success would have ended the revenue stream.
Failure extended it.

Fictional clarity became scalable.
It became repeatable.
It became predictable.

And the architecture remained untouched.

The Internalization of Fictional Clarity

Inside the enterprise, fictional clarity evolved from a coping mechanism into a survival strategy.

A senior leader once admitted privately, “I don’t know what this role is supposed to do.”
Then, in the next meeting, he introduced the role with confidence.

Teams learned to hide behind titles.
Boards learned to hide behind language.
Executives learned to hide behind vocabulary.

Fictional clarity became a shared delusion.

It allowed the organization to feel modern without becoming modern.
It allowed the architecture to remain untouched while appearing responsive.
It allowed leaders to feel decisive without making decisions.

The danger of fictional clarity is not that it misleads.
The danger is that it satisfies.

It gives the organization just enough confidence to avoid confronting the real work.
It creates the belief that naming the work is the same as understanding it.
It creates the illusion that the presence of a role is equivalent to the presence of capability.

The CAIO is the newest beneficiary of fictional clarity.
It inherits a title that sounds powerful and a mandate that sounds strategic.
It inherits expectations that exceed its position in the hierarchy.
It inherits the ambiguity that sustains the ecosystem around it.
It inherits the responsibility leadership refuses to carry.

It inherits the burden of transformation without the authority to transform.

The CAIO is not a new idea.
It is the newest expression of fictional clarity.

The Bridge to the Architecture

Fictional clarity does not end when the title is assigned.
It does not resolve when the mandate is announced.
It persists because the system requires it.

It survives because the architecture cannot absorb the truth.
It thrives because the organization would rather rename the work than redesign the structure that makes the work impossible.

Fictional clarity is not a communication problem.
It is not a leadership problem.
It is not a talent problem.

It is an architectural inevitability.

It is the operating system beneath every failed transformation.
It is the logic behind every role that collapses under the weight of expectations it was never designed to carry.
It is the reason organizations repeat the same mistakes with the same confidence and the same outcome.

The CAIO is simply the newest expression of this pattern.
A title created to absorb the anxiety of change.
A role designed to carry responsibility without authority.
A function built to signal transformation without requiring it.

The system has done this before.
It will do it again.
It will continue until the architecture itself is confronted.

The same mechanism that produces fictional clarity eventually produces something more dangerous: false precision.
Fictional clarity is the language that allows the organization to feel certain without being certain.
False precision is the numbers, dates, and forecasts that allow the organization to act as if that certainty were real.
Both are expressions of the same architectural need, to collapse ambiguity into something that looks like

control without changing the structure that makes control impossible.

This chapter ends where the next begins.

To understand why roles fail, we must understand the system that produces them.
To understand why transformations collapse, we must understand the architecture that refuses to change.
To understand why fictional clarity persists, we must understand the structure that makes it inevitable.

Chapter 3 begins that work.
It is not a continuation.
It is an exposure, and it started with the creation of the Project Manager.

Once language became the organization's primary tool for avoiding structural decisions, it needed a human vessel to carry that ambiguity. The first sacrificial role emerged not from strategy, but from the architecture's need for a place to put the work it refused to own.

CHAPTER 3

The Moment the Pattern Becomes Visible (1990s)

The first cracks appeared quietly.

A global manufacturer had just launched its most ambitious product line in a decade.
The engineering team was behind schedule.
Operations was overwhelmed.
Marketing was demanding dates no one could commit to.
The architecture, built for a slower, simpler era, was buckling under the weight of work that crossed every functional boundary.

A meeting was called.
The VP of Engineering arrived with a stack of printouts.
The VP of Operations arrived with a list of escalations.
The VP of Marketing arrived with a deadline circled in red.
No one owned the whole picture.
No one could.

The CEO listened as each leader described a different version of the same problem.
Dependencies no one controlled.
Priorities no one aligned.
Decisions no one could make.
The architecture was being asked to carry a load it was never designed to bear.

The CEO finally said, "We need someone to coordinate this."

The room exhaled.
A role had been named.
The pressure had somewhere to go.

The first project manager was hired two weeks later.

He walked into a system that had already decided his fate.

He was responsible for everything.
He owned nothing.

This was the moment the pattern became visible—the moment the enterprise discovered it could avoid structural change by creating a role to absorb the pressure.

The PM was the first sacrificial role.
The architecture recognized it long before the organization did.

The Rise of the PM (the first sacrificial role)

The PM's first week was a tour of contradictions.

He was told he would "drive alignment," but no one reported to him.
He was told he would "manage dependencies," but the dependencies were created by decisions made far above his pay grade.
He was told he would "ensure delivery," but he had no authority to change priorities, staffing, or scope.

He sat in a cross-functional meeting where engineering refused to commit to dates, operations refused to adjust capacity, and marketing refused to move the launch.
All eyes turned to him.

"Can you bring this together?" someone asked.

He nodded, because what else could he do.

He asked for scope.
The organization handed him velocity.
He asked for decisions.
The steering committee offered ceremony.
He asked for clarity.
The framework supplied artifacts.
He asked what success meant.
The dashboard displayed motion.
He asked who owned the outcome.
Everyone pointed at the process.

He worked nights.
He worked weekends.
He worked across functions that had no incentive to cooperate.

He was praised for his effort.
He was blamed for the outcome.

The PM was the first attempt to use human effort to compensate for architectural insufficiency.

The role did not fail.
The architecture did.

But the organization interpreted the failure as a lack of maturity.

And so the next move was inevitable.

The Birth of the PMO (fictional governance)

The PM's struggle was visible.
The architecture's failure was not.

Leaders saw missed deadlines.
They did not see structural impossibility.

They saw inconsistent reporting.
They did not see decision rights scattered across the hierarchy.

They saw cross-functional friction.
They did not see incentives pulling teams in opposite directions.

So they created an office.

The PMO was framed as the function that would bring discipline to chaos, standardize delivery, and create predictability across work that crossed functional boundaries.

It promised visibility.
It promised alignment.
It promised control.

But the PMO did not own the levers that create control.

It owned the artifacts that simulate it.

It produced templates, not authority.
It produced dashboards, not decisions.
It produced governance rituals, not governance power.

In its first month, the PMO created a reporting cadence.
In its second month, it created a risk register.
In its third month, it created a dashboard.

None of it changed the architecture.

The PMO became the first fictional governance function—
a structure that looked like oversight but lacked the structural position required to govern anything.

It created the appearance of order without altering the conditions that produced disorder.

This was the moment the enterprise learned a dangerous lesson:

If a problem is structural, create a function that reports on it instead of redesigning the system that causes it.

The Misdiagnosis (the profession grows while the architecture stays still)

The PMO struggled.
The architecture remained untouched.

Executives interpreted the struggle as a failure of discipline.
Consultants interpreted it as a market opportunity.
PMI interpreted it as a profession.

Inside PMI headquarters, a committee debated the outline of a new certification.
They discussed process groups, knowledge areas, and maturity levels.
They debated terminology.
They refined vocabulary.

No one asked whether the architecture made any of it possible.

The certification legitimized the role without empowering it.

The curriculum standardized the language without changing the system.
The body of knowledge created the appearance of rigor without addressing the structural conditions that made rigor impossible.

The profession grew.
The architecture did not.

Organizations concluded the PMO needed more process.
More templates.
More checkpoints.
More reporting.
More oversight.

They did not conclude the architecture needed to change.

The misdiagnosis became the foundation of the next thirty years.

The PM and PMO were not anomalies.
They were prototypes.

The Pattern Becomes a System

Once the PM and PMO became normalized, the architecture learned a new behavior.

It learned that it could survive pressure without changing.
It learned that it could absorb complexity without redesigning itself.
It learned that it could protect power structures without confronting the limits of the operating model.

It learned that roles could be used as structural insulation.

A new problem emerged.
A new role was created.
The role was given responsibility without authority.
The role failed for structural reasons.
The failure was interpreted as a lack of maturity.
A new role was created to replace it.

The cycle continued.

Inside one enterprise, the sequence played out in a single year.

A PM failed.
A PMO was created.
The PMO failed.
A "Transformation Office" was created.
The Transformation Office failed.
A "Strategic Execution Office" was created.

Each new role inherited the same structural impossibility.
Each new role entered the same architecture.
Each new role carried the same burden.

The organization believed it was evolving.
It was repeating.

The vocabulary became more sophisticated.
The architecture stayed the same.

The failure of the PM and PMO did not teach the organization anything; it taught the market everything.
The architecture's refusal became a commercial opportunity, and the consulting ecosystem industrialized the workaround.

The Inheritance (how every future role absorbed the same structural impossibility)

The PM and PMO did not simply fail.
They created a template for failure.

Once the architecture learned that it could protect itself by creating roles that absorbed structural tension, every future wave of complexity triggered the same response.

Data became a problem.
A Chief Data Officer was created.

Innovation became a problem.
A Chief Innovation Officer was created.

Transformation became a problem.
A Chief Transformation Officer was created.

AI became a problem.
A Chief AI Officer was created.

Each role entered the same architecture.
Each role inherited the same structural impossibility.
Each role was celebrated at creation and isolated at execution.

The enterprise believed it was evolving.
It was not.

It was repeating the same architectural mistake with increasing confidence.

The PM and PMO were the first sacrificial roles.
They were the prototypes for a lineage of roles designed to absorb the consequences of architectural avoidance.

They revealed the truth the organization still refuses to confront:

You cannot delegate structural decisions to roles that do not own the structure.

This chapter ends with the recognition that the PM and PMO were not the end of the pattern.
They were the beginning.

The next chapter follows the pattern forward into the consulting era, where fictional clarity became a commercial engine and the manufacturing of roles became an industry.

CHAPTER 4

The Room Where Fiction Became a Product

The room was too bright for what was about to happen.
Fluorescent light flattened everything, faces, intentions, the truth.
A U-shaped table framed the space, the kind of layout designed to suggest collaboration while preserving hierarchy.
At the front of the room, a projector hummed with the low, steady confidence of a machine that had done this a thousand times before.

On the screen, a slide waited in silence.

Digital Transformation Roadmap — Phase 0 Assessment

No one in the room had seen the slide before.
Everyone pretended they had.

The executives filed in with the practiced choreography of people who had been through too many reviews.
They carried laptops they would not open, notebooks they would not use, and expressions calibrated to appear engaged without revealing uncertainty.

The consultants were already seated.

The partner sat at the center, flanked by two directors, each with a stack of printed frameworks arranged like offerings.
The analysts sat behind them, typing notes that would become the justification for the next phase of the engagement.

The partner clicked the remote.

A four-quadrant model.
A maturity curve.
A color-coded heat map.

The executives nodded.
Not because they understood, because nodding was safer than asking.

The partner spoke in the language of fictional clarity: sentences that sounded decisive but revealed nothing, frameworks that implied structure without describing it, recommendations that gestured toward transformation without requiring it.

The architecture of the enterprise was never mentioned.
It never is.

Then the partner advanced to the slide that mattered.

Recommended Executive Role: Chief Digital Officer

The room shifted.
Not visibly.
Structurally.

The executives leaned forward just enough to signal interest.
The consultants paused just long enough to signal importance.
The architecture remained untouched just long enough to signal inevitability.

The partner explained that the CDO would "own the digital agenda," "drive cross-functional alignment," and "accelerate transformation."

No one asked the question that would have ended the meeting.

What authority will this role have?

Instead, they asked the questions that preserved the fiction.

Where should the role report?
What should the first 100 days look like?
What capabilities will the role need?

The partner answered each question with the confidence of someone who understood the architecture better than the people who ran it.

He knew the CDO could not succeed.
He also knew the CDO would need help.

That was the business model.

The meeting ended with a sense of progress.
The executives felt reassured.
The consultants felt victorious.
The architecture felt nothing.

The slide deck was printed.
The role was approved.
The engagement was extended.

This was the room where fictional clarity became a product.
This was the moment the consulting era industrialized the creation of roles.

How the Workaround Became a Market

By the early 2000s, the workaround that began with the PM and PMO had matured into something larger than any single role. It had become a market.

Organizations were struggling with digital disruption, globalization, and the early waves of automation. The environment was shifting faster than the architecture, but the structural decisions required to respond were too costly, too slow, and too politically dangerous.

Leaders needed a way to appear decisive without confronting the architecture that made decisiveness impossible.

Consultants offered the perfect solution.

They offered roles.

Inside a consulting firm's leadership meeting, a partner pointed to a spike in client inquiries.

"Everyone wants digital," he said. "They don't know what it means. That's the opportunity."

The room nodded.

The CDO was framed as the executive who would modernize the enterprise, transform the customer experience, and integrate digital capabilities across the organization.

It sounded bold.
It sounded strategic.
It sounded like leadership.

But the role entered the same architecture that had rejected the PM and PMO.

It entered without ownership of systems.
It entered without control of budgets.
It entered without authority over engineering.
It entered without influence over incentives.

The CDO was responsible for outcomes that required structural decisions it could not make.

Consultants didn't need the CDO to succeed.
They needed the CDO to exist.

A role without definition created demand for interpretation.
A role without boundaries created demand for operating models.
A role without authority created demand for escalation pathways.

That was the business model.

Frameworks.
Assessments.
Roadmaps.
Capability models.

Ambiguity became a product.
Ambiguity became a service.
Ambiguity became a subscription.

The consulting era did not invent fictional clarity.
It industrialized it.

The Industrialization of Fictional Clarity

By the time the consulting era reached full maturity, fictional clarity was no longer an organizational reflex. It was a supply chain.

A repeatable, scalable, revenue-generating system for manufacturing roles that sounded decisive while preserving the architecture that made decisiveness impossible.

The PM and PMO had proven the model.
The CDO made it profitable.
The market did the rest.

Inside a strategy practice, a director reviewed a draft of a white paper titled *The Future of Innovation Leadership*. It introduced a role that did not yet exist.

“Chief Innovation Officer,” he said. “This will land.”

The team refined the language.
The keynote was drafted.
The maturity model was built.
The diagnostic was packaged.

By the time the role reached the executive team, it already had:

a framework

a capability map

a transformation roadmap

a recommended operating cadence

It arrived pre-packaged, pre-validated, and pre-monetized.

The organization believed it was adopting a solution.
In reality, it was adopting a product.

The CINO entered the same architecture that had rejected every role before it.

It entered without control of resources.
It entered without influence over priorities.
It entered without authority over execution.

Innovation became a theater.
The CINO became the curator of ideas that could not survive contact with the system.

Consultants built innovation labs.
They built ideation workshops.
They built "future readiness" assessments.

Ambiguity was not a flaw.
It was the fuel.

The ecosystem reinforced itself.
The architecture remained untouched.

This was the industrialization of fictional clarity.
Not a moment.
A machine.

The Roles That Could Not Survive the Architecture

The consulting era did not merely create roles.
It created roles that were structurally doomed the moment they were named.

The Chief Transformation Officer was the clearest expression of the pattern.

It was created to lead change that required decisions only the CEO could make.
It was created to coordinate functions that were not structurally aligned.
It was created to deliver outcomes that required the redesign of incentives, reporting lines, and power structures.

None of these were within its control.

Inside one enterprise, the CTO presented a transformation roadmap to the executive team.
It required changes to funding models, decision rights, and cross-functional governance.

The CEO nodded.
The CFO hesitated.
The COO resisted.
The architecture held.

The CTO became the place where impossible expectations accumulated.
It became the executive embodiment of the original sin: transformation delegated to a title so the architecture would not have to change.

The CTO was not alone.

The CDO was responsible for modernizing systems it did not own.
The CINO was responsible for innovation it could not fund.
The Chief Experience Officer was responsible for customer outcomes shaped by functions it could not influence.
The Chief Strategy Officer was responsible for

alignment in organizations structurally incapable of aligning.

Each role inherited the same contradiction.
Each role entered the same architecture.
Each role carried the same burden of responsibility without authority.

Consultants understood this better than anyone.

The more the roles struggled, the more support they required.
The more support they required, the more consulting hours could be sold.
The more hours sold, the more the architecture remained untouched.

This was not incompetence.
This was not immaturity.
This was not a failure of talent.

This was the system working exactly as designed.

The Normalization of Avoidance

By the 2010s, avoidance was no longer a workaround.
It was doctrine.

Organizations learned that they could:

delegate transformation to a role

outsource responsibility to consultants

purchase the appearance of progress

avoid altering the architecture that made progress impossible

Inside a board meeting, a director asked why the digital transformation was behind schedule.

The CEO responded, “We’re bringing in additional support.”

No one asked whether the architecture was the problem.
They asked whether the roadmap needed refinement.

Inside a leadership review, the CINO presented a portfolio of ideas.
None were funded.
The room applauded the creativity.

Inside a transformation office, a team updated a dashboard that showed progress no one could feel.

The architecture remained untouched.

Avoidance became operationalized.
Ambiguity became normalized.
Failure became expected.

The cycle no longer required interpretation.
It simply ran.

The consulting era taught organizations that transformation could be performed symbolically.
It taught leaders that responsibility could be outsourced.
It taught boards that progress could be measured through language rather than outcomes.

The PM and PMO were the prototypes.
The consulting era turned the prototype into a

product.
The product became a market.
The market became a system.

The CAIO as the Latest Release

The consulting era ends where the present begins.

Not with a breakthrough.
Not with a structural shift.
Not with a moment of architectural reckoning.

It ends with the newest role in the lineage of fictional clarity, the Chief AI Officer.

The CAIO did not emerge from necessity.
It emerged from the same market forces that produced the CDO, the CINO, and the CTO.

It is not a response to AI.
It is a response to anxiety.

The CAIO inherits the same ambiguity.
It inherits the same structural impossibility.
It inherits the same commercial ecosystem.
It enters the same architecture.

It is framed as the executive who will lead the AI agenda, modernize the enterprise, and integrate AI capabilities across every function.

But the role enters without ownership of data.
It enters without control of engineering.
It enters without authority over incentives.
It enters without influence over the systems that determine whether AI can be adopted at all.

The CAIO is responsible for outcomes that require structural decisions it cannot make.

Consultants understand this dynamic better than anyone.

They have already built the frameworks.
They have already built the assessments.
They have already built the roadmaps.
They have already built the capability models.

The product is ready.
The market is primed.
The architecture is unchanged.

The CAIO is not an anomaly.
It is the next release in a product line that began with the PM and PMO.
It is the newest vessel for the same avoidance.
It is the most recent expression of the belief that transformation can be delegated to a title.

The consulting era industrialized fictional clarity.
The CAIO is its latest artifact.

This chapter ends with the recognition that the pattern has reached its limit.

The roles have become too large.
The expectations too unrealistic.
The architecture too exposed.

The next chapter turns to the system itself.
Not the roles it produces.
The architecture that makes those roles impossible.

Chapter 5 begins the confrontation the enterprise has avoided for three decades.
Because once the roles reach their limit, only the architecture remains.

CHAPTER 5

The Architecture Beneath the Org Chart

The executive team gathered around a long table polished to a mirror shine.
A freshly printed org chart lay in front of each person, still warm from the copier.
Boxes, lines, reporting structures, clean, legible, comforting.
The CEO tapped the page with the confidence of someone who believed the diagram reflected reality.

"This is our structure," he said.

The CHRO nodded.
The CFO adjusted her glasses.
The COO leaned back, arms crossed.

Everyone stared at the chart as if it were a map.
It wasn't.

The real architecture revealed itself in the next ten minutes.

A director raised a question about a cross-functional initiative.
The COO answered before the VP responsible could speak.
The CFO interrupted to clarify budget implications.
The CHRO reminded the room that headcount approvals still flowed through her office.
The CEO nodded, not because he agreed, but because he knew the escalation would land on his desk anyway.

The org chart said one thing.
The architecture said another.

The architecture beneath the org chart is not a diagram.
It is the set of constraints that determines what the system can and cannot do.
It decides which decisions are possible, which are delayed, which are avoided, and which are never even perceived.
Titles sit on top of it.
Roles inherit it.
No mandate can escape it.

The architecture lived in the way decisions moved, slowly, upward, through layers of leaders who owned pieces of the work but not the whole.
It lived in the way budgets were defended like territory.
It lived in the way functions negotiated influence instead of outcomes.
It lived in the way no one could act without someone else's permission.

The architecture was not documented.
It was enacted.

It was older than the strategy.
Older than the leadership team.
Older than the transformation program they were pretending to discuss.

The org chart was a story.
The architecture was the truth.

And the truth was simple:
before any role enters the enterprise, the architecture has already decided its fate.

The Commitments That Hold the Architecture in Place

A week later, the CEO convened a meeting to discuss "accelerating decision-making."
The irony was immediate.

The first commitment revealed itself when the CIO proposed distributing authority for certain technology decisions.
The CFO stiffened. "We can't decentralize spend," she said. "It creates risk."
Centralized authority was not a preference.
It was a structural commitment.

The second commitment surfaced when the VP of Sales pushed back on a cross-functional initiative.
"My team can't take on additional reporting," he said. "We have our own priorities."
Functional sovereignty was not an organizational quirk.
It was a territorial boundary.

The third commitment appeared when a conflict emerged between Operations and Product.
Instead of resolving it, both leaders escalated upward.
The CEO sighed. "I'll decide."
Hierarchical escalation was not a habit.
It was the architecture's circulatory system.

The fourth commitment showed up when the CFO reminded the room that budget ownership determined decision rights. "If I fund it," she said, "I approve it."
Budgets were not financial instruments.
They were political ones.

The fifth commitment became visible when the COO argued against changing a long-standing process.
"We need predictability," he said. "We can't keep shifting."
Predictability over adaptability was not a performance preference.
It was a survival instinct.

These commitments were not written anywhere.
They didn't need to be.

They lived in the reflexes of leaders who had succeeded within the system.
They lived in the incentives that rewarded stability over evolution.
They lived in the boundaries that defined who could say yes and who could say no.

A role could challenge a workflow.
A role could challenge a process.
A role could challenge a practice.

But a role could not challenge the commitments that held the architecture in place.

This was the system the CAIO would inherit.
Not a blank canvas.
A fortified structure.

The Constraints Every Role Inherits

A newly hired Chief Transformation Officer sat in her office reviewing her mandate.
The language was bold.
The expectations were sweeping.
The architecture was silent.

Her first week revealed the truth.

She asked for authority to realign priorities across functions.
She was told to "influence."

She asked for clarity on who owned cross-functional decisions.
She was told "it depends."

She asked for the ability to shift budget to fund transformation.
She was told "that's not how we operate."

The first constraint was the boundary of authority.
She was responsible for outcomes she could not decide.

The second constraint was the boundary of incentives.
She needed system-level alignment.
Functions were rewarded for local optimization.

The third constraint was the boundary of ownership.
She was positioned as the leader of transformation.
She owned none of the systems required to transform anything.

She tried to move the work forward.
The architecture absorbed her effort like sand absorbing water.

She escalated decisions.
The hierarchy slowed them.

She pushed for alignment.
Functions defended their territory.

She proposed structural changes.
The CFO reminded her that budgets were fixed.

She wasn't failing.
She was discovering the constraints every transformational role inherits.

The architecture did not oppose her.
It simply refused to move.

How the Architecture Protects Itself

The CTO's first major initiative stalled within a month.
Not because the idea was flawed, but because the architecture activated its defenses.

Distributed accountability ensured no one owned the full problem.
Engineering blamed Product.
Product blamed Operations.
Operations blamed Finance.

Centralized authority ensured decisions moved upward.
The CEO became the bottleneck.
The CTO became the messenger.

Incentive misalignment ensured no function would sacrifice its metrics for system-level outcomes.
Sales protected its pipeline.
Operations protected its throughput.
Finance protected its budget.

Narrative displacement ensured the architecture escaped scrutiny.
The story became one of "resistance," "culture," and "leadership gaps."

Role substitution ensured the system never had to confront itself.
When the CTO struggled, the organization created a

"Transformation Office."
When the Transformation Office struggled, they created a "Strategic Execution Office."

The architecture remained untouched.

These mechanisms did not require coordination.
They were emergent.
Predictable.
Self-reinforcing.

The architecture did not defend itself through force.
It defended itself through design.

This was the system the CAIO would inherit.
A system that protects itself long before it protects the role.

There is a point in every system where behavior stops being the primary lever.
Meetings, mandates, and new roles lose their ability to change outcomes because the architecture has already decided how the system will behave.
That point, the moment when structure, not behavior, becomes the dominant determinant of what happens next, is the beginning of the structural turn.
Most organizations reach it long before they realize it exists.

The Misdiagnosis That Protects the Architecture

A board meeting was called to review why the transformation was behind schedule.

The CHRO blamed culture.
The COO blamed execution.

The CFO blamed prioritization.
The CEO blamed communication.

No one blamed the architecture.

The first misdiagnosis was cultural resistance.
"People aren't embracing the change."

The second was skill deficiency.
"We need more training."

The third was leadership failure.
"We need stronger sponsorship."

The fourth was role clarity.
"We need to refine the mandate."

Each explanation was comforting.
Each explanation was familiar.
Each explanation was wrong.

The architecture ensured failure would be interpreted as a human problem, not a structural one.

The board left the meeting believing the solution was to "strengthen the role."

The architecture left the meeting untouched.

This was the system's most effective defense:
it convinced the organization to diagnose the wrong problem every time.

The Role That Cannot Escape the Architecture

Every transformational role enters the enterprise with the same promise:

to modernize, to integrate, to accelerate, to align, to transform.

And every transformational role enters the enterprise with the same constraint:
the architecture that never changes.

The PM believed coordination could overcome fragmentation.
The PMO believed governance could overcome misalignment.
The CDO believed digital could overcome legacy systems.
The CINO believed innovation could overcome inertia.
The CTO believed transformation could overcome hierarchy.

Each role believed it was different.
Each role believed it had a mandate.
Each role believed it had sponsorship.
Each role believed it had urgency.

None of them understood the architecture they were walking into.

They did not inherit authority.
They inherited contradictions.

They did not inherit power.
They inherited expectations.

They did not inherit a system designed for change.
They inherited a system designed to survive change.

The architecture that never changes does not oppose these roles.
It absorbs them.

It uses them.
It outlives them.

It allows them to signal progress without enabling them to produce it.
It allows them to coordinate without allowing them to decide.
It allows them to influence without allowing them to alter the structure.
It allows them to exist without allowing them to succeed.

This is the original sin of organizational transformation:
roles are created to absorb responsibility, not to redistribute power.

And this is the architecture the CAIO inherits.

Not a modernized system.
Not a redesigned enterprise.
Not a structure prepared for AI.

But the same architecture that defeated every role before it.

The CAIO is not entering a new era.
The CAIO is entering the next iteration of an old pattern.

The next chapter reveals why the CAIO is not a governance innovation, not a strategic breakthrough, not a structural evolution, but the latest expression of a system that refuses to change.

The CAIO is not the exception.
The CAIO is the next release.

Once the architecture is visible, the illusion of novelty collapses.
The CAIO enters not as a breakthrough, but as the latest vessel for the same structural impossibility.

CHAPTER 6

The Role That Arrives Before the Work

The CAIO does not enter a modernized enterprise.
It enters the same architecture that defeated every role before it.

Not a breakthrough.
A continuation.

A new title created to absorb pressure the hierarchy refuses to confront.
A new vessel for responsibility the structure refuses to carry.
A new symbol of progress that requires no structural change.

The CAIO arrives the way every role arrives:
with urgency, with vocabulary, with expectation.

It does not arrive with authority.

The architecture remains intact.
The hierarchy remains untouched.
The incentives remain misaligned.

The CAIO enters a system that has already decided the limits of the role.

The Mandate Without Ownership

The CAIO is positioned to "drive transformation."
To "accelerate AI adoption."
To "modernize decision-making."
To "integrate intelligence across the enterprise."

Each phrase implies power.
None of them grant it.

The CAIO is positioned to inherit responsibility without ownership.
Expectations without leverage.
Accountability without authority.

The architecture retains the decision rights.
The hierarchy retains the incentives.
The system retains the constraints.

The CAIO inherits the burden.

This is not a new pattern.
It is the next iteration of an old one.

The Ecosystem That Forms Around Ambiguity

Around the CAIO, the ecosystem moves quickly.

Consultants build frameworks.
Analysts build categories.
Associations build credentials.
Vendors build roadmaps.
Boards build expectations.

The ecosystem does not need the CAIO to succeed.
It needs the CAIO to exist.

Ambiguity creates demand.
Demand creates products.
Products create markets.

The CAIO becomes the newest center of gravity for fictional clarity —
a role defined more by the anxiety it absorbs than the authority it possesses.

The ecosystem flourishes.
The architecture remains untouched.

The Inheritance of Impossibility

The CAIO enters a system designed for local optimization, not enterprise coherence.
A system where incentives reward fragmentation, not integration.
A system where decision rights are scattered across functions that do not want to relinquish them.
A system where governance is ceremonial, not structural.
A system where architecture determines outcomes long before roles are created.

The CAIO is positioned to inherit the same impossibility that every role before it inherited.

Not because the CAIO lacks capability.
Not because the CAIO lacks clarity.
Not because the CAIO lacks vision.

But because the architecture lacks change.

The Illusion of Novelty

The CAIO is framed as innovation.
As modernization.
As evolution.

But novelty is not determined by vocabulary.
Novelty is determined by architecture.

And the architecture has not changed.

The CAIO is not a governance innovation.
Not a strategic breakthrough.
Not a structural evolution.

It is the next vessel for avoidance.

The next symbolic gesture.
The next attempt to name the work without owning it.
The next role created to absorb responsibility the hierarchy refuses to carry.

The CAIO does not represent a new era.
It represents the next release of an old pattern.

The Pattern That Repeats

Every role created to "drive transformation" enters with the same structural disadvantage:

Responsibility without authority.
Expectations without ownership.
Accountability without power.
Mandates without structural position.

The CAIO is positioned to inherit all of it.

Not as an exception.
As the next release.

The architecture remains.
The pattern remains.
The outcomes remain.

The Architecture That Absorbs The Caio

The architecture does not resist the CAIO.
It absorbs it.

It absorbs the vocabulary.
It absorbs the mandate.
It absorbs the urgency.

It does not absorb the work.

The CAIO enters with language that sounds decisive.
The architecture converts that language into symbolism.

The CAIO enters with expectations that sound transformative.
The architecture converts those expectations into ceremony.

The CAIO enters with a mandate that sounds structural.
The architecture converts that mandate into narrative.

Nothing changes because nothing is allowed to change.

The architecture protects itself by neutralizing the role that threatens to expose it.
Not through conflict.
Through absorption.

The CAIO becomes part of the structure it was created to challenge.
Not by choice.
By design.

The architecture has learned how to survive new roles.
It survives them by converting them into the next expression of avoidance.

The CAIO is positioned to inherit that conversion.

The System That Reproduces Itself Through The Caio

The system does not wait for the CAIO to act.
It acts around the CAIO.

Consultants position the CAIO as a buyer.
Analysts position the CAIO as a category.
Vendors position the CAIO as a budget line.
Boards position the CAIO as reassurance.

The CAIO becomes the newest justification for the loop.
The newest vessel for fictional clarity.
The newest placeholder for structural decisions the hierarchy refuses to make.

The CAIO does not disrupt the system.
It extends it.

It extends the belief that naming the work is the same as owning it.
It extends the belief that assigning responsibility is the same as granting authority.
It extends the belief that transformation is a role, not a decision.

The system reproduces itself by producing the next role that will inherit impossibility.
The CAIO is positioned to be that role.

Not because the CAIO is flawed.
Because the system is unchanged.

The Consequence Of Introducing The Caio

The consequence of introducing the CAIO is not transformation.
It is repetition.

The CAIO becomes the next chapter in a lineage of roles created to carry burdens the architecture refuses to confront.
The next symbol of progress that requires no structural change.
The next narrative of modernization that protects the hierarchy from redistribution of power.

The CAIO does not alter the architecture.
It reveals it.

It reveals the refusal to redesign decision rights.
It reveals the refusal to confront incentives.
It reveals the refusal to change the structure that determines outcomes.

The CAIO is positioned to expose the architecture by inheriting its impossibility.

This is the consequence.
This is the pattern.
This is the inevitability.

The Bridge to the Loop

The CAIO does not fail because of AI.
It fails because of architecture.

It does not struggle because of technology.
It struggles because of incentives.

It does not collapse because of complexity.
It collapses because decision rights remain unchanged.

The CAIO is not defeated by the future.
It is defeated by the past.

The next chapter reveals how the architecture reproduces itself —
how the loop sustains the system,
how the system sustains the loop,
and how every new role becomes the next vessel for structural impossibility.

The CAIO is not a breakthrough.
It is the continuation.

The architecture remains.
The loop remains.
The pattern remains.

CHAPTER 7

The loop does not begin in a meeting.
It begins in the architecture.
Long before anyone clicks to a slide or debates a dependency, the system has already chosen its load path.
The loop is not a behavioral failure or a leadership weakness.
It is the structural inevitability that emerges when responsibility is assigned to roles and authority remains in the architecture.
Every meeting that follows is simply the moment the system reveals the decision it has already made.

A matrix structure is the quiet architect of this inevitability.
It creates two chains of command that cannot be reconciled, two definitions of success that cannot be harmonized, and two sources of authority that cannot be resolved.
The organization believes it has designed flexibility, but what it has actually manufactured is structural ambiguity.
No one owns the work, no one owns the decision, and no one owns the consequences.
The Loop is not a behavioral failure.
It is the physics of a governance surface that was never matched with a governance system.

The Meeting Where the Loop Reproduces Itself

The consultant clicked to the first slide.
"Thanks for making the time," he said, though no one had a choice.
"We're here to discuss the leadership structure for the next phase."

No one mentioned the role that had just collapsed.
They didn't need to.
The empty chair at the table carried the memory of it.

The COO broke the silence.
"We can't stall again. We need someone who can actually move this forward."

The CIO nodded.
"Someone with authority across functions. Someone who can cut through the noise."

The consultant advanced the slide.
A new title appeared in the center of a diagram.

"Chief AI Officer," he said.
"Positioned to drive enterprise-wide transformation."

The room shifted.
Not excitement.
Relief.

A new title meant a new narrative.

The CFO leaned back.
"Will this role finally solve the fragmentation problem?"

The consultant smiled the way consultants do when the answer is already scripted.
"With the right mandate, yes."

The VP of HR tapped her pen.
"We'll need a competency model. And a maturity framework. And probably a credentialing path."

The CEO stared at the slide as if it were a lifeline.
"We need someone who can bring this all together," he said.

He had said the same sentence two years earlier about the role that had just failed.

The PMO director didn't speak.
She didn't need to.
She had watched the last role inherit responsibility without authority, expectations without support, accountability without ownership.

She knew what would happen next.
Everyone in the room did.

But no one said it.

The consultant moved to the next slide.
"We can draft the job description this week. We'll outline the mandate, the decision rights, the cross-functional responsibilities."

The CIO nodded.
"Good. Let's move quickly."

The architecture stayed silent.
It always does.

The CEO closed his laptop.
"Let's proceed."

And that was it.
The loop had reproduced itself.
A new role would inherit the same impossibility as the last one.

The collapse was already scheduled.

The system had protected itself again.

What the Room Reveals

The meeting looked like a decision-making session.
It wasn't.
It was a ritual.

A ritual organizations perform when they need to convert discomfort into motion without confronting the source of the discomfort.

The collapse of the previous role should have forced a structural conversation.
It didn't.
It never does.

The system has learned how to redirect pressure before it reaches the architecture.

The room did not gather to understand what failed.
It gathered to name what would fail next.

The new title was not a solution.
It was a release valve.

It allowed the organization to feel decisive without making a single structural decision.

Every person in the room played a part:

Executives asked questions that implied authority they would never grant.

The consultant offered frameworks that implied clarity the architecture could not support.

HR proposed legitimacy mechanisms that implied definition where none existed.

No one lied.
No one manipulated.
No one acted with bad intent.

The system simply guided everyone toward the conclusion it always produces.

The new role would inherit responsibility without authority.
It would inherit expectations without support.
It would inherit accountability without ownership.

The collapse was already embedded in the design.

This is how the loop sustains itself.
Not through incompetence.
Not through malice.
Through relief.

The relief of believing the next role will succeed where the last one failed.
The relief of avoiding the structural decisions that would make success possible.

The room did not choose the loop.
The architecture chose it for them.

The people simply followed the path of least resistance —
the path the system has reinforced for years.

The loop is not optional.
It is the default path the architecture takes when pressure increases and no structural decision is made.
That is why it appears in every sector, under every mandate, with different titles and the same outcome.
The loop is the architecture, behaving as designed.

How the Loop Sustains Itself

The loop does not survive because people believe in it.
It survives because it asks nothing of the architecture.

It offers the organization a way to feel responsive without becoming responsible.

Every new role begins with a promise:

This time will be different.
This time the mandate will be clear.
This time the authority will be real.
This time the system will align.

The promise lasts just long enough to justify the creation of the role.

Then the architecture takes over.

The new leader enters with urgency.
They meet with every function.
They listen.
They diagnose.
They map the landscape.

They identify the decisions that must be made.
They discover none of those decisions belong to them.

The organization responds with encouragement.

“We support you.”
“We’re aligned.”
“This is critical.”

Everyone agrees the work is important.
No one changes anything.

The role becomes the place where unresolved decisions accumulate.
The place where conflicting priorities converge.
The place where expectations land when the system has nowhere else to put them.

The leader escalates.
The escalation circulates.
The decision evaporates.

The stall begins.

The organization interprets the stall as a failure of execution.
It never interprets it as a failure of design.

The architecture remains invisible.
The role becomes the explanation.

The loop tightens.

The leader becomes overwhelmed.
The mandate becomes impossible.
The narrative shifts.

The role is no longer the solution.
The role is now the problem.

The collapse becomes inevitable long before it becomes visible.

And when the collapse arrives, the system does not pause.
It does not reflect.
It does not examine the architecture.

It simply prepares the next role.
The next promise.
The next cycle.

The loop sustains itself by converting structural failure into personal failure.
Architectural impossibility into individual inadequacy.
Systemic avoidance into a story about the wrong hire.

The system never blames itself.
It never needs to.

The loop provides a new character for the next act.

The Market That Forms Around the Loop

Across town, an analyst firm hosted a briefing titled **"Emerging Leadership Roles in the Age of AI."**

The room was full.
It always was when a new title entered the market.

"We're seeing a clear trend," the analyst said. "Organizations are appointing Chief AI Officers to accelerate transformation."

She didn't mention most of those roles were less than a year old.
She didn't need to.

A CIO raised his hand.
"Is this role actually working anywhere?"

The analyst smiled.
"It's early," she said.
"But the momentum is undeniable."

Momentum was easier to sell than outcomes.

Down the hall, a professional association convened a working session to design a certification for the same role.

Strategy.
Governance.
Ethics.
Innovation.

Competencies were added to the whiteboard with the confidence of people who had never seen the role succeed.

Across the city, a consulting firm held an internal call.

"Clients are asking about the CAIO," the partner said. "We need a point of view."

A manager shared a draft framework.
A director suggested a maturity model.
A senior associate proposed a diagnostic.

The partner approved all of it.

No one questioned whether the role could succeed.
That wasn't the point.

The point was to be ready when the next collapse created the next wave of demand.

None of these rooms coordinated with each other.
They didn't need to.

They were all responding to the same signal:

A new role had entered the loop.

The organization wanted clarity.
The market wanted relevance.
The architecture wanted nothing at all.

And yet, all three moved in perfect alignment.

The People Inside the Loop

The announcement went out on a Tuesday morning.

A new role.
A new mandate.
A new phase.

Teams read it the way they read every announcement.

Some skimmed.
Some shrugged.
Some forwarded it with a single line:
"Here we go again."

In one department, a manager stared at her screen. She had lived through three versions of this role already.

Each one arrived with urgency.
Each one left quietly.

Her team asked, "What does this mean for us?"

She gave the answer she always gave.
"We'll know more soon."

Down the hall, a product lead felt a different kind of fatigue.
He had spent a year trying to get decisions no one would make.

Now those decisions would be routed to someone new.

He didn't expect the outcome to change.
Only the inbox.

In another building, a data scientist forwarded the announcement to a colleague with a single emoji.

They had watched the last role attempt to fix problems older than both of them.

They didn't doubt the new leader's intelligence.
They doubted the system's willingness to let anyone succeed.

Across the organization, reactions were small and private.

A raised eyebrow.
A quiet laugh.
A resigned nod.

Not cynicism.
Recognition.

They had seen the loop enough times to know its rhythm.

The loop didn't need their belief.
It only needed their familiarity.

And it had that already.

The Loop as Governance

The new leader arrived two weeks later.

Not with fanfare.
With meetings.

In one early session, she asked, "Who makes the final call on this?"

The room went quiet.

Not confused.
Not defensive.
Just quiet in the way rooms get when the answer is structurally inconvenient.

"It depends," someone said.

"Depends on what?"

Another pause.

"On who's asking."

Later, she asked about decision rights.
A slide appeared with arrows pointing in every direction.

Shared accountability.
Distributed ownership.
Cross-functional alignment.

Words that sounded collaborative but behaved like fog.

She met with the PMO director.
They reviewed a portfolio of stalled initiatives.

"Would escalation help," she asked.

The PMO director shook her head.
"Escalation only works when someone wants to own

the decision.
Here, escalation is just another form of circulation."

By the end of the month, she had mapped the responsibilities assigned to her role.
She had also mapped the authority required to fulfill them.

The two diagrams did not overlap.
Not even slightly.

She brought this to the CEO.
He agreed with every point.
He thanked her for the clarity.

Then he asked her to "keep pushing forward" while he "socialized the implications."

She left the meeting knowing what that meant.

The architecture was not going to change.
The loop was already tightening around her.

The system didn't need to resist her directly.
It only needed to remain itself.

And it would.

The Design Beneath the Loop

By the end of the quarter, the new leader had settled into a rhythm.

Not the rhythm she expected.
The rhythm the system imposed.

Meetings that clarified nothing.
Decisions that moved nowhere.

Escalations that circled back to the same people who had avoided the decisions in the first place.

In a cross-functional review, she asked, "What is the actual blocker here."

A director answered immediately.
"We don't have alignment."

"Alignment on what?"

Another pause.

"On who decides."

Later, she met with the PMO director again.
They reviewed the same stalled initiatives.

"This is where every role like yours gets stuck," the PMO director said.
"Right here."

"Why doesn't anyone fix it?" the new leader asked.

"Because the system works for the people it was designed to protect."

It wasn't cynicism.
It was clarity.

"So the loop isn't an accident."

"No," the PMO director said.
"It's governance."

The word landed quietly.
Not dramatic.
Just true.

The loop wasn't malfunctioning.
It was functioning exactly as designed.

The Enterprise as a Loop-Producing Machine

By the end of the fiscal year, the organization looked exactly as it had before the new role arrived.

The charts were updated.
The language had shifted.
The slide templates had been refreshed.

But the structure, the real structure, had not moved at all.

In a leadership meeting, the CEO referenced the new role as evidence of progress.

"We're building momentum," he said.

Everyone nodded.
Everyone understood the performance.
Everyone participated in it.

Outside the room, teams adjusted to the new reporting lines the way they always did.

Some complied.
Some ignored them.
Most waited to see which version of the structure would survive the quarter.

They had learned the architecture was not what the org chart said.
It was what the system enforced.

One afternoon, the new leader walked past a wall of framed posters from previous transformation efforts.

Each one had a slogan.
Each one had a timeline.
Each one had a champion.

None of them had survived.

She paused, studying the dates.

The posters formed a quiet archive of the loop.

Not a history of failure.
A history of repetition.

Later that week, she met with the PMO director again.

"This is where the system holds," the PMO director said, pointing to a line on the dashboard.

The new leader understood.

The loop wasn't a cycle.
It was a boundary.

A boundary the architecture would not cross.
A boundary the organization would not challenge.
A boundary the market would not question.

The loop wasn't a symptom.
It wasn't a mistake.
It wasn't a failure.

It was the operating model.

And until the architecture changed, the loop would continue —
quietly, predictably, relentlessly —
producing the next role, the next collapse, the next justification, the next cycle.

The system didn't need to defend itself.
It only needed to persist.

And it would.

The Moment Governance Reveals Itself

The loop is not an accident.
It is a system.
It is the mechanism through which the architecture protects itself and the mechanism through which avoidance becomes operational.
It is how the enterprise sustains the appearance of progress without disturbing the structure that resists it.

The next chapter examines the deeper physics of this refusal —
why the architecture preserves itself,
why leaders hesitate at the edge of structural decisions,
and why the system continues to reproduce the same pattern with the same confidence and the same outcome.

The loop persists not because people fail, but because deeper forces hold it in place. To understand why the loop reproduces itself, we must examine the physics of refusal.

CHAPTER 8

The forces that govern refusal are not external pressures acting on the organization.
They are behaviors the system generates from inside its own architecture.
Structural inertia, power preservation, incentive misalignment, narrative comfort, and distributed accountability are not things that "happen to" the enterprise.
They are the way the enterprise behaves when its constraints are left untouched.
The forces are endogenous.
They are the architecture expressing itself.

The First Force: Structural Inertia

The executive team gathered for the quarterly strategy review.
The agenda was familiar.
The choreography was familiar.
The outcome was already written.

Halfway through the session, the COO presented a slide titled **Structural Implications**. Three decisions.
Real decisions.
Structural ones.

The room went quiet.

The CEO studied the slide.
"These are significant moves."

"They're necessary," the COO said.

Silence followed.
Not resistance.

Not disagreement.
Something heavier.

The CFO broke it first.
"We should model the impact."

The CHRO added, "We'll need to socialize this."

The CIO suggested a working group.
The CMO suggested a pilot.
The strategy lead suggested a phased approach.

The COO closed his laptop.
He had seen this pattern before.

Everyone agreed the decisions were important.
No one wanted to be the one to make them.

The CEO finally said,
"Let's revisit this next quarter. We need more clarity."

The slide disappeared.
The meeting moved on.
The structure remained untouched.

Later, the COO walked past a wall of old org charts.
Different shapes.
Same architecture.

The organization wasn't avoiding change because it was confused.
It was avoiding change because the cost of altering the structure was higher than the cost of repeating the cycle.

Structural inertia wasn't emotional.
It wasn't personal.
It wasn't intentional.

It was physics.

The Second Force: Power Preservation

The steering committee met on a Thursday morning.
A meeting designed for decisions.
A meeting where decisions rarely happened.

The transformation lead presented a proposal to shift ownership of a critical initiative.
A small change on paper.
A seismic one in practice.

The rationale was clear.
The benefits were clear.
The risks of doing nothing were clear.

The room listened politely.

Operations spoke first.
"This makes sense. But we need to understand the downstream impact."

Product nodded.
"And the resource implications."

Finance added,
"And the budget alignment."

HR added,
"And the talent implications."

IT added,
"And the governance model."

Everyone agreed the change was logical.
Everyone also understood what it meant:

Authority would shift.
Priorities would shift.
Influence would shift.

Power would move.

The transformation lead tried again.
"We can't keep delaying this. The current structure is blocking progress."

No one disagreed.
Agreement was never the issue.

Operations leaned forward.
"Let's take this offline."

A smaller group meant the same people.
The same conversations.
The same outcome.

The CEO intervened.
"Let's revisit this next month. We need alignment."

The transformation lead closed her laptop.
She didn't argue.

Resistance rarely arrived as a no.
It arrived as a pause.
A deferral.
A request for more clarity.

Later, she told a colleague,
"They're not blocking it. They're just not letting it move."

"That's how power protects itself," he said.

Not malicious.
Not dramatic.
Not conscious.

Just physics.

Power didn't need to fight change.
It only needed to wait.

The Third Force: Incentive Misalignment

The quarterly business review was running long.
It always did when numbers were involved.

The head of Sales walked the room through his pipeline.
Strong quarter.
Stronger forecast.
Predictability.
Stability.
Repeatability.

Words that landed well in a room where bonuses depended on them.

When he finished, the COO shifted the conversation.
"We need to accelerate the new initiative."

Sales nodded politely.
"Of course. As long as it doesn't jeopardize this quarter's numbers."

Finance agreed.
"We need to protect the run rate."

Product added,
"We can't disrupt the roadmap."

Operations added,
"We can't introduce variability."

Every function had a reason to delay.
Every reason was rational.
Every rational reason pointed in the same direction:

Not now.

The CEO pushed.
"We've been talking about this for months."

Sales smiled.
"We'll support it, as long as it doesn't impact our targets."

Targets tied to compensation.
Compensation tied to predictability.
Predictability tied to avoiding risk.

The transformation lead wrote in her notebook:

The system rewards the opposite of what it asks for.

After the meeting, she told the CFO,
"We can't transform if everyone is incentivized to maintain the status quo."

The CFO didn't disagree.
"We can't change incentives mid-year."

The elevator doors closed.

"And even if we could," she added quietly,
"I'm not sure anyone would want us to."

Not resistance.
Not sabotage.
Not fear.

Alignment, perfect alignment, with the incentives the system had built.

Transformation required risk.
The system rewarded avoiding it.

Incentive misalignment didn't block change.
It redirected it back into the familiar.

The Fourth Force: Narrative Comfort

The communications team prepared the quarterly town hall.
The theme was "Accelerating Transformation."
The same theme as last quarter.
And the quarter before that.

The director of Communications edited a sentence.
"We should emphasize momentum."

The strategy lead nodded.
"We are making progress. Just not the kind we can measure yet."

The transformation lead watched the edits accumulate.
Clarity.
Alignment.
Acceleration.

Words that sounded decisive.
Words that described nothing specific.

She finally spoke.
"We haven't resolved any of the structural blockers.
Shouldn't we acknowledge that."

The room went still.
Not hostile.
Just uncomfortable.

"We need to reinforce confidence," Communications said.
"People need a story they can believe in."

"If we focus on the blockers," Strategy added,
"we'll lose the room."

Later, during the town hall, the CEO delivered the remarks exactly as written.
The audience nodded.
They applauded.
The narrative worked.

Afterward, two managers walked back to their desks.

"Sounds like we're moving fast."
"Sounds like we're saying we're moving fast."

Not cynicism.
Fluency.

The transformation lead wrote in her notebook:

The story is easier to change than the structure.

Narrative comfort didn't block transformation. It replaced it.

The Fifth Force: Distributed Accountability

The cross-functional working session began with good intentions.
It always did.

Representatives from every major function sat around the table.
Product.
Engineering.
Operations.
Finance.
HR.
Legal.
PMO.

The facilitator opened with a slide titled **Decision Needed**.

Everyone nodded.
Everyone agreed.
Everyone waited for someone else to make it.

The transformation lead walked through the issue.
Clear dependencies.
Clear risks.
Clear options.

"Who owns this decision?" she asked.

Silence.

Product said,
"We can't move until Engineering signs off."

Engineering said,
"We can't sign off until Operations confirms capacity."

Operations said,
"We can't confirm capacity until Finance approves budget."

Finance said,
"We can't finalize budget until Legal reviews compliance."

Legal said,
"We can't assess compliance until HR defines the talent plan."

HR said,
"We can't define the talent plan until Product finalizes scope."

The circle closed.
Perfectly.
Effortlessly.
Predictably.

The CEO joined halfway through.
He listened to the loop.
He asked,
"Who is accountable for the outcome?"

Silence again.

Finally, the PMO director said,
"Technically, all of us."

The CEO nodded.
"And when all of you are accountable," he said, "none of you are."

The meeting ended with action items.
Every action item depended on someone else's action item.

The loop was complete.

The transformation lead wrote:

Distributed accountability isn't a gap. It's a shield.

The Forces Converge

The executive team reconvened for another strategy checkpoint.
Same room.
Same table.
Same agenda.

The COO opened.
"We're still blocked."

No one looked surprised.

Structural inertia had delayed decisions.
Power preservation had softened urgency.
Incentive misalignment had redirected attention.
Narrative comfort had reframed stagnation as momentum.
Distributed accountability had ensured no one owned the outcome.

The forces didn't operate in sequence.
They operated in concert.

The CEO said,
"We need to break through this."

The transformation lead watched the faces around the table.
Agreement without commitment.
Support without ownership.
Momentum without movement.

The CFO suggested another review.
The CHRO suggested another alignment session.
The CIO suggested another pilot.
Strategy suggested another narrative.

The COO closed his laptop.
"We're not stuck because we lack ideas," he said.
"We're stuck because the system is doing exactly what it was built to do."

Silence.
Not defensive.
Not confrontational.
Just structural.

The CEO asked,
"So what do we do?"

The transformation lead said,
"We stop pretending the blockers are operational.
They're architectural."

No one disagreed.
No one volunteered to change the architecture either.

The meeting ended with next steps.
Every step avoided the structure.
Every step preserved the system.

Later, she wrote:

The system doesn't refuse change. It refuses the cost of change.

The Loop Reproduced

The next portfolio review took place in a smaller room.

Fewer people.
Same pattern.

The transformation lead presented an updated timeline.
Progress where progress didn't matter.
No movement where movement was required.

The COO said,
"We're slipping again."

Product said,
"Dependencies."

Engineering said,
"Capacity."

Finance said,
"Budget."

HR said,
"Talent."

The CEO asked,
"What do you need from us?"

She hesitated.
Not because she didn't know.
Because she knew the answer wouldn't land.

"I need structural decisions," she said.
"Not more coordination."

The room went still.

Operations said,
"We can't make structural changes mid-cycle."

Finance said,
"We can't disrupt the forecast."

HR said,
"We can't destabilize the teams."

IT said,
"We can't introduce risk."

Strategy said,
"We can't shift the narrative."

The CEO said,
"So we stay the course."

Everyone nodded.

After the meeting, she walked past a wall of posters from previous initiatives.
Different slogans.
Different champions.
Same outcome.

She wrote:

The forces don't resist change. They reproduce the loop.

Refusal as Operating Principle

Refusal operates at more than one layer.
At the surface, it looks like leaders declining to make hard decisions, teams avoiding structural clarity, boards postponing uncomfortable conversations.
Beneath that, refusal is architectural: the system routes pressure away from the places where change would alter power, incentives, or capital.
What looks like personal hesitation is often the architecture defending itself.

The board met at the end of the quarter.
Polished decks.
Controlled expressions.

The CEO presented the transformation update.
The narrative was crisp.
The charts were clean.
The story was coherent.

The board nodded.
They knew the difference between progress and the appearance of progress.
They also knew the architecture.
They had approved it.
They benefited from it.

A board member asked,
"What's preventing acceleration?"

The CEO said,
"We're working through structural considerations."

No one asked which structures.
No one asked who owned them.
No one asked what it would cost to change them.

After the meeting, the CEO told the transformation lead,
"Good work on the narrative."

She said,
"Narrative isn't the problem."

He didn't disagree.
He didn't agree.
He simply walked away.

She returned to her office and looked at the whiteboard.

Arrows.
Loops.
Dependencies.
Forces.

None of it was accidental.
None of it was personal.
None of it was emotional.

It was structural.

Structural inertia kept the system stable.
Power preservation kept leaders aligned with the status quo.
Incentive misalignment kept risk at bay.
Narrative comfort kept the story intact.
Distributed accountability kept responsibility diffuse.

Together, they formed a closed system.
A system that absorbed pressure.
A system that neutralized disruption.
A system that reproduced the loop with precision.

Refusal wasn't a behavior.
It wasn't a mindset.
It wasn't a failure.

It was the operating principle of the enterprise.

And until the architecture changed, the refusal would continue —
quietly, predictably, relentlessly.

The system didn't need to resist transformation.
It only needed to remain itself.

The Moment the Forces Become Architecture

Refusal is not a behavior.
It is a system.
It is the architecture's way of protecting itself from the cost of structural change and the mechanism through which the loop is reproduced with precision.
It is how the enterprise sustains continuity while appearing to pursue transformation.

The next chapter examines what it takes to break this pattern,
the conditions under which real architectural change becomes possible, why those conditions are so rarely present,
and what must shift for an organization to escape the loop it continues to recreate.

Refusal is not emotional or cultural, it is architectural.
And once the architecture is exposed, the organization faces a choice it can no longer defer: redesign the structure or repeat the loop.

CHAPTER 9

The Moment the Loop Breaks Through

The executive offsite was held at a quiet resort an hour outside the city.
Neutral ground.
No conference rooms.
No org charts.
Just a long table, a stack of printed decks, and a leadership team that had run out of ways to explain the lack of progress.

The CEO opened with a familiar line.
"We need to understand why we're not moving faster."

No one responded.
Not because they disagreed.
Because they had said everything there was to say.

The COO flipped through the deck.
Stalled initiatives.
Unresolved dependencies.
Deferred decisions.
The same patterns.
The same explanations.
The same outcomes.

Product spoke first.
"We've added roles. We've added programs. We've added frameworks. Nothing is changing."

Finance added,
"We're spending more and getting the same result."

HR added,
"Teams are exhausted. They don't believe the next initiative will be different."

IT added,
"We're optimizing around the same constraints."

The CEO listened.
He had heard versions of this before.
But something in the room was different.
The tone.
The posture.
The absence of performance.

The transformation lead stood at the far end of the table.
She had been quiet all morning.
She wasn't waiting for her turn.
She was waiting for the moment when the truth could be spoken without being dismissed as pessimism.

She walked to the whiteboard and drew a simple loop.
No labels.
No arrows.
Just the shape.

"This is what we're doing," she said.

The room watched her.
No one interrupted.

"We keep creating roles to solve problems the structure won't let them solve.
We keep launching initiatives the architecture won't support.
We keep asking for outcomes the system isn't designed to produce."

She paused.
No one looked away.

"This isn't a coordination problem," she said.
"It's an architectural one."

The COO nodded.
The CFO exhaled.
The CHRO closed her notebook.
The CEO leaned back.

For the first time, no one offered a workaround.
No one suggested a pilot.
No one proposed a new role.

The room wasn't resisting the truth.
It was finally ready to hear it.

The loop wasn't failing.
The architecture was.

And the cost of pretending otherwise had finally exceeded the cost of confronting it.

The First Requirement: A Structural Decision

After lunch, the leadership team reconvened.
The morning had stripped away the usual defenses.
No one was pretending the cycle was a misunderstanding.

The CEO stood at the whiteboard.
"If this is the system," he said, "then what breaks it?"

"A structural decision," the transformation lead said.

The COO nodded.
"Which one."

She pointed to the org chart projected on the wall. "This one. Ownership of the initiative has to move. The current structure can't deliver the outcome."

Product shifted.
"That's a major change."

Finance added,
"It affects budget authority."

HR added,
"And reporting lines."

IT added,
"And governance."

The CEO looked around the room.
"We've been avoiding this for months."

No one disagreed.

"We keep trying to solve a structural problem with operational tools," the transformation lead said. "It won't work. Someone has to own the outcome with the authority to make the decisions required to achieve it."

Silence.
Not resistance.
Recognition.

The COO finally spoke.
"If we do this, it will disrupt half the organization."

"That's what structural change does," she said.

Finance exhaled.
"We'll take a hit on predictability."

HR added,
"And on stability."

The CEO looked at each of them.
"We're already taking a hit. We're just not admitting it."

He turned back to the whiteboard.
"So who owns it."

Silence again.
Not because they didn't know.
Because they did.

The COO raised his hand.
"I'll take it. But only if the authority comes with it."

"It will," the CEO said.

It wasn't dramatic.
It wasn't triumphant.
It wasn't even optimistic.

It was simply the first real decision the organization had made in months.

A structural decision.
Not a role.
Not a narrative.
Not a workaround.

Something had moved that wasn't symbolic.

Every failed transformation is a collision between ambition and capacity.
Ambition is narrative, the story the organization tells itself about what it will do, how fast it will move, how much it will change.
Capacity is physics, the actual constraints of

architecture, capital, time, and attention.
Governance collapses when narrative exceeds physics and no one is willing to reduce the story to match the system's real load-bearing ability.

The Second Requirement: Clarity of Ownership

The next morning, the leadership team gathered in a smaller room.
No slides.
No agenda.
Just a question on the whiteboard:

Who owns the outcomes we keep missing?

The COO sat at the head of the table.
He had accepted ownership of the initiative the day before.
But one decision wasn't enough.
The system had too many places to hide.

"We can't break the cycle unless every outcome has a single owner," the transformation lead said.
"Not a committee. Not a working group. Not a coordinating role."

Product leaned forward.
"We've always shared ownership. It keeps things collaborative."

"Shared ownership is how we avoid decisions," she said.
"Collaboration isn't the problem. Diffusion is."

Finance tapped her pen.
"If we assign single owners, we'll expose the gaps."

"That's the point."

The CEO nodded.
"Let's start with the top five outcomes."

The room shifted.
Not tense.
Just alert.

The COO took the first.
"This belongs with me. And I'll take the authority that comes with it."

Product took the second.
"This one is ours. But we need decision rights clarified."

Finance took the third.
"Finance owns this. But we need the metrics aligned."

IT took the fourth.
"We'll take it. But only if we can redesign the approval chain."

The fifth outcome sat untouched.
Everyone looked at it.
Everyone knew what it represented:

The cross-functional work no one wanted to own because owning it meant confronting the architecture directly.

The CEO asked,
"Who owns this?"

Silence.

"This is the one that always collapses," the transformation lead said.

“Because no one owns it. Because everyone touches it. Because the structure wasn’t designed for it.”

The COO exhaled.
“If we don’t assign it, the loop continues.”

“Then assign it,” the CEO said.

Operations raised her hand.
“I’ll take it. But only if we redesign the interfaces around it.”

“That’s what ownership requires,” the transformation lead said.

The CEO wrote her name on the board.
A simple gesture.
A structural shift.

Ownership wasn’t a slogan.
It wasn’t a slide.
It wasn’t a principle.

It was a structural act.

And for the first time, the organization was making one.

The Third Requirement: Coherence

Two weeks later, the leadership team met again.
The structural decisions were rippling through the organization.
Reporting lines shifting.
Teams unsettled.
Leaders recalibrating.

The COO opened.
"Ownership is clearer. But we're still running into contradictions."

The transformation lead nodded.
Contradictions weren't mistakes.
They were artifacts of an architecture built through years of incremental decisions.

Product spoke first.
"We're being asked to accelerate experimentation. But our metrics still reward predictability."

Finance added,
"We're being asked to collaborate across functions, but the budget model reinforces silos."

IT added,
"We're being asked to move faster, but the approval chain hasn't changed."

HR added,
"We're being asked to redesign roles, but the compensation structure still reflects the old hierarchy."

The CEO listened.
He wasn't surprised.
He had lived inside these contradictions for years.

The transformation lead walked to the whiteboard and wrote four words:

Structure
Incentives
Metrics
Decision Rights

"These have to align," she said.
"If even one pulls in a different direction, the system will revert."

Product nodded.
"We can't ask teams to innovate when the metrics punish variance."

Finance added,
"We can't ask leaders to collaborate when the incentives reward local optimization."

IT added,
"We can't ask for speed when every decision requires four signatures."

HR added,
"We can't ask for new behaviors when the structure reinforces the old ones."

The CEO asked,
"So what do we change first?"

"The contradictions," she said.
"All of them. At the same time."

Silence.
Not because the idea was radical.
Because it was true.

Coherence wasn't a principle.
It wasn't a value.
It wasn't a slide.

It was the alignment of the system with itself.

And for the first time, the system was beginning to move in one direction instead of five.

The Fourth Requirement: Commitment

The first structural changes went live on a Monday.
New reporting lines.
New owners.
New expectations.

By Wednesday, the pressure surfaced.

Operations walked into the CEO's office.
"Teams are confused. They want to know why we're doing this now."

"Because we said we would," he said.

"Some leaders want to slow down."

"Do you think we should?"

"No. But they're uncomfortable."

"So are we."

Across the hall, Finance met with the transformation lead.
"We're getting pushback on the new incentive model. People are worried about losing predictability."

"Predictability is what kept us stuck."

"This is going to get noisy."

"Noise is the price of redesign."

Later, the COO told the CEO,
"Some leaders want to create a coordinating role to smooth the transition."

"No," the CEO said.
"No new roles. No buffers. No fictional clarity."

"Then we hold."

"We hold."

The transformation lead entered.
"This is the part where organizations usually retreat," she said.
"They make a few structural moves, feel the discomfort, and then create a role to absorb it."

"Not this time," the CEO said.

"Then say it out loud," she said.
"To the whole team."

The next morning, the CEO opened the leadership meeting with one sentence:

"We are not going back."

The room went quiet.

"We made structural changes. They will be uncomfortable. They will disrupt patterns. They will challenge identities. That is the work. We are not creating a role to carry the burden. We are carrying it."

Commitment wasn't enthusiasm.
It wasn't confidence.
It wasn't a speech.

It was staying with the discomfort long enough for the architecture to shift.

And for the first time, the organization wasn't looking for a way out.
It was looking for a way through.

The Fifth Requirement: Patience

The first month felt like turbulence.
Teams adjusting.
Leaders learning.
The organization wasn't resisting the new architecture.
It was learning how to live inside it.

Operations asked,
"When will this settle?"

"It won't settle quickly," the transformation lead said.

"They're used to initiatives. They're used to timelines. They're used to things ending."

"This isn't ending," she said.
"It's becoming."

Finance asked,
"When will we see the impact?"

"Not this quarter. Maybe not next quarter."

"Then how do we know it's working?"

"Because we're finally aligning the system with the outcomes we want."

Later, the CEO and transformation lead walked the operations floor.
People were adjusting.
Slowly.

Unevenly.
But adjusting.

A manager approached.
"We're trying to adjust to the new decision rights. It's taking time."

"It should," the CEO said.

"Are we moving too slowly."

"No," she said.
"We're moving at the speed of redesign."

The CEO paused.
"I didn't expect it to feel like this."

"Like what."

"Like we're rebuilding the plane while flying it."

"That's what structural change is."

"How long until this feels normal?"

"Months. Maybe longer."

"And that's okay?"

"It has to be."

Patience wasn't waiting.
It wasn't hoping.
It wasn't endurance.

It was reinforcing the new architecture through consistent decisions long enough for the system to internalize it.

And for the first time, the organization wasn't rushing to declare victory.
It was learning how to live inside the change it had chosen.

The Sixth Requirement: Honesty

By the second month, the organization had settled into an uneasy rhythm.
The structure was in place.
The owners were making decisions.
The contradictions were being dismantled.

But something deeper hadn't shifted.

The transformation lead saw it in every meeting:
the hesitation,
the careful phrasing,
the instinct to soften the truth.

In a review session, the COO said,
"We're making progress. Slowly."

"What's slowing us down?" the CEO asked.

"Teams are still adjusting."

"Say it," the transformation lead said quietly.

The COO exhaled.
"Some leaders are still operating the old way. They're saying the right things, but they're not making the decisions the new structure requires."

"Why not?" the CEO asked.

"Because they don't believe we'll stay with this. They think we'll revert."

The room went still.

Finance entered.
"Teams are waiting for the old incentives to return."

HR entered.
"Some leaders are waiting for the old reporting lines to return."

The CEO closed his notebook.
"Then we confront it."

"Honesty isn't blame," the transformation lead said. "It's naming the architecture we actually have, not the one we wish we had."

They walked into the larger conference room.
The extended leadership team was waiting.

The CEO didn't use slides.
He didn't use narrative comfort.

He spoke plainly.

"We are not going back.
The old architecture is not returning.
The loop is not returning.
If you are waiting for the system to revert, it won't."

Silence.
Not shock.
Not anger.
Just confrontation.

Honesty wasn't catharsis.
It wasn't confession.
It wasn't vulnerability.

It was alignment with reality.

And for the first time, the organization wasn't pretending the architecture was something it wasn't.

It was seeing itself clearly.

The literacy required for architectural change exists at two levels.
The first is individual literacy, the ability of leaders and practitioners to see the system beneath the org chart and name the constraints that actually govern behavior.
The second is system literacy, the ability of the organization to behave as if those constraints are real, to route decisions through architecture instead of titles.
Without individual literacy, the system cannot be seen.
Without system literacy, the system cannot change.

The System Rebuilt

By the end of the quarter, the organization felt different.
Not fixed.
Not transformed.
Just different in the way a structure feels when its foundations have been moved and the walls haven't caught up yet.

The leadership team gathered for a final review.
No old decks.
No talking points.
No performance layer.

Operations opened.
"The new owners are making decisions. Real ones."

Finance added,
"The incentives are starting to shift behavior."

HR added,
"Teams are adjusting to the new reporting lines."

IT added,
"The approval chain is collapsing."

Product added,
"The contradictions are disappearing."

The CEO listened.
He wasn't looking for momentum.
He was looking for alignment.

The transformation lead watched the room.
She could see the architecture settling into its new shape.
Slowly.
Unevenly.
But undeniably.

The CEO asked,
"Are we breaking the cycle?"

She looked at the whiteboard where the loop had once been drawn.
The board was clean now.
Not because the loop had vanished —
but because the organization had stopped pretending it didn't exist.

"We're doing the only thing that breaks it," she said.
"We're redesigning the system."

Operations leaned forward.
"So this is what real transformation feels like?"

"It feels like work," she said.

Finance added,
"It feels like consequence."

HR added,
"It feels like discomfort."

IT added,
"It feels like clarity."

The CEO closed his notebook.
"It feels like the truth."

Breaking the cycle wasn't inspiration.
It wasn't insight.
It wasn't a heroic role.

It was the slow, deliberate, structural reconfiguration of the enterprise.

And the organization had finally begun it.

Collapse has always had two layers.
The first is governance collapse, the moment the rituals, roles, and frameworks can no longer hide the gap between responsibility and authority.
The second is structural collapse, the moment the architecture itself is forced to reveal that it cannot deliver the outcomes it has been promising.
Volume 1 lives mostly in the first layer.
The second layer is already present.
It simply has not been named yet.

The Moment the Architecture Requires Ownership

Breaking the cycle is not an act of will or optimism or narrative strength.
It is the slow, deliberate reconstruction of the architecture itself, carried through decisions that disrupt the system and held long enough for the organization to internalize them.
It is the moment when leaders stop asking the structure to behave differently and begin redesigning it to produce the outcomes they claim to want.

The next chapter examines what emerges on the other side of this shift:
an operating model that no longer relies on roles to absorb contradictions, no longer depends on fictional clarity to maintain momentum, and no longer treats transformation as an event.

It is the beginning of a system built to sustain clarity rather than collapse under it.

When an organization finally confronts the architecture, the illusions that once protected it begin to collapse.
The next chapter shows what happens when fictional clarity can no longer sustain the system.

CHAPTER 10

When the Language Stops Working

It happened on an ordinary Tuesday.

The executive team gathered for the quarterly transformation update.
The deck was polished.
The language was familiar.

"Accelerate."
"Align."
"Clarify."

Words that had carried the organization through years of initiatives.

But something in the room had shifted.

The COO flipped to the next slide.
"We're seeing momentum," he said.

No one nodded.

Product scanned the page.
"Momentum where?"

The COO hesitated.
"In the narrative."

Finance closed her laptop.
"Narrative isn't progress."

The transformation lead watched the exchange.
She had felt this moment approaching for months —
the slow erosion of belief,
the widening gap between language and reality,

the quiet recognition that the tools the organization had relied on no longer worked.

The CEO tried again.
"We're building the foundation for long-term success."

HR shook her head.
"We've said that for three years."

IT added,
"And the blockers haven't moved."

The room went still.
Not confrontational.
Not dramatic.
Just still in the way rooms get when the story no longer holds.

"The language isn't landing anymore," the transformation lead said.

The CEO looked at her.
"What do you mean?"

She turned the deck toward him.
"These words used to create alignment.
Now they create distance.
People hear them and assume nothing is changing."

Finance nodded.
"We've exhausted the vocabulary."

Operations added,
"We've exhausted the frameworks."

Product added,
"We've exhausted the titles."

The CEO leaned back.
"So what's left?"

The transformation lead drew a small circle on the whiteboard.
"The structure," she said.
"It's the only thing that still determines the outcome."

No one argued.
No one tried to rescue the narrative.
No one reached for a new slogan.

The room wasn't rejecting the language.
It had simply stopped believing in it.

Fictional clarity didn't collapse.
It eroded.

And on that Tuesday morning, the erosion finally became visible.

When Naming Stops Working

Two days later, the CEO held a town hall.
It was meant to reset momentum.
The comms team had prepared the usual talking points.

Renewed focus.
Sharpened priorities.
Clarified roles.

The script was polished.
The cadence was familiar.

But the room didn't respond the way it used to.

When the CEO introduced the new **Transformation Alignment Office**, the audience didn't lean forward.
They didn't nod.
They didn't take notes.

They just listened with the quiet patience of people who had heard this before.

"This office will ensure cross-functional clarity," he said.

A manager whispered,
"We already had one of those."

Her colleague whispered back,
"We've had three."

The CEO moved to the next slide.
"A new framework to streamline decision-making."

Someone in the back muttered,
"Frameworks don't make decisions."

The transformation lead watched the room.
Not cynical.
Just awake.

The CEO opened the floor for questions.
A senior engineer raised his hand.

"We've renamed this work four times," he said.
"What's actually changing?"

Silence.
Not tense.
Not rebellious.
Just honest.

The CEO hesitated.
He looked at the transformation lead.

She stepped forward.
"The names aren't the change," she said.
"The structure is."

The engineer nodded slowly.
"Then why are we still naming things?"

"Because naming used to work," she said.
"It doesn't anymore."

Another employee asked,
"So what should we expect?"

"Expect fewer announcements," she said.
"Expect fewer frameworks.
Expect fewer titles.
Expect more decisions that change how the system actually works."

The CEO watched the room.
He could feel the shift.

The narrative wasn't collapsing.
It was losing its utility.

Fictional clarity didn't end with a crisis.
It ended with a question the old language couldn't answer.

When Roles Stop Working

A week later, the CEO met with a group of directors.
It was supposed to be a check-in on the new structure.
Instead, it became something else.

"My team keeps asking what the new title means,"
one director said.
"I don't know what to tell them."

Another added,
"People assume the title comes with authority it doesn't have."

A third said,
"And some think the title replaces the structural changes we're making."

The COO entered mid-conversation.
"Operations is seeing confusion too.
People think the new roles *are* the transformation."

Finance added,
"Leaders are asking whether the new titles change decision rights."

HR closed her notebook.
"They don't.
But they think they do."

The room went quiet.

"This is the erosion," the transformation lead said.
"Roles used to carry symbolic power.
They used to signal change.
They used to create momentum."

She paused.

"But now the organization knows better."

The CEO frowned.
"Knows what?"

"That a title doesn't change the architecture," she said.
"And they're right."

"So what do we do?" a director asked.

"We stop treating roles as substitutes for structure," she said.
"We stop naming our way out of architectural decisions.
We stop pretending a title can compensate for a system that refuses to change."

The CEO stood.
"We're not using titles to signal transformation anymore," he said.
"We're using structure."

A director asked,
"So what do we tell our teams?"

"Tell them the role doesn't define the work," the CEO said.
"The architecture does."

Fictional clarity didn't end with a declaration.
It ended when the organization stopped believing that roles could do the work of structure.

When Frameworks Stop Working

The strategy team met on a Friday afternoon to review the new **Enterprise Maturity Model**. Clean stages.
Crisp labels.
A sense of progression.

The room had seen dozens of versions over the years.

But this time, the energy was different.

"We're between Stage Two and Stage Three," the strategist said.
"With the new structure, we can accelerate toward Stage Four."

No one reacted.

"What changes between the stages?" the COO asked.

The strategist hesitated.
"Mindsets. Behaviors. Ways of working."

Finance closed her binder.
"Those aren't structural."

"They're directional," the strategist said.

"Directional isn't architectural," the transformation lead said.

Silence.

Product spoke next.
"We've been 'between stages' for five years.
Nothing in this model changes incentives.
Nothing changes decision rights.
Nothing changes ownership."

"It gives us a shared language," the strategist said.

"We don't need language," IT said.
"We need decisions."

"And reinforcement," HR added.

The CEO closed his laptop.
"We're not doing this anymore."

"Not doing what," the strategist asked.

"Pretending a framework can move the architecture."

The transformation lead nodded.
"Frameworks used to create the appearance of progress.
Now they reveal the absence of it."

"So what replaces it?" the strategist asked.

"Structure," Operations said.
"Incentives," Finance said.
"Decision rights," HR said.
"Ownership," IT said.
"Alignment," Product said.

The strategist looked down at the model.
"So what's the point of this?"

"There isn't one," the transformation lead said.

Fictional clarity didn't end with a failure.
It ended when the organization stopped believing that frameworks could substitute for structural decisions.

When the Ecosystem Stops Working

A major consulting firm arrived to pitch a new operating model.
Partners.
Directors.
A hundred-slide deck.

"We've identified a maturity gap," the partner said.
"Our model moves organizations from Level Three to Level Five in eighteen months."

No one reacted.

“We recommend establishing a Transformation Governance Office,” he continued.

“What structural decisions does it make?” the CEO asked.

“It coordinates.”

“Coordinates what?” the COO asked.

“Alignment.”

“We don’t need alignment theater,” Finance said.

The partner shifted.
“We also recommend a new role, Chief Transformation Architect.”

“We’re not manufacturing roles anymore,” HR said.

“This role would accelerate your maturity progression.”

“We’re not progressing through stages,” IT said.
“We’re redesigning the system.”

The partner looked at the transformation lead.
She didn’t rescue him.

“We’re not buying clarity,” she said.
“We’re building architecture.”

“So what exactly are you looking for?” he asked.

“Structural support,” the CEO said.
“Not symbolic action.”

The partner closed his laptop.
"We may need to rethink our approach."

The ecosystem didn't collapse.
It simply lost its leverage.

Fictional clarity had powered it for decades.
Once the organization stopped believing in symbolic clarity, the ecosystem's influence evaporated.

When the Conditions Finally Change

By the third month, the organization had stopped looking for shortcuts.
The language had quieted.
The frameworks had disappeared.
The titles had settled into the background.

What remained was the architecture —
exposed, imperfect, visible.

The leadership team gathered for a quarterly review.
The agenda was short.

Is the system capable of producing the outcomes we want.

Operations spoke first.
"We're seeing early signs.
Not everywhere.
Not consistently.
But the work is moving."

Finance nodded.
"The incentives are starting to shift behavior."

HR added,
"Teams aren't asking for the old reporting lines back."

IT added,
"Decisions are happening faster."

Product added,
"The contradictions are fewer."

The CEO listened.
He wasn't looking for celebration.
He was looking for coherence.

"Are we transforming?" he asked the transformation lead.

She shook her head.
"Not yet."

The room steadied.

"Transformation isn't the outcome of ending fictional clarity," she said.
"It's what becomes possible after it ends."

"So what do we have now?" the COO asked.

"Conditions," she said.
"For the first time, the architecture isn't fighting the outcomes."

"But it's not producing them yet," Finance said.

"It won't," she said.
"Not until the new structure is reinforced through a hundred decisions we haven't made yet."

"So we're at the beginning," HR said.

"Yes," she said.
"For the first time."

The CEO nodded.
"Then we stay with it."

The organization wasn't mistaking clarity for maturity anymore.
It wasn't mistaking naming for design.
It wasn't mistaking narrative for structure.

It understood that the end of fictional clarity wasn't the finish line.
It was the starting point.

When the Organization Finally Sees Itself

The leadership team met one last time before the quarter closed.
Not for a review.
Not for a decision.

Just to look at the system they had rebuilt —
not finished,
not polished,
but undeniably different.

They gathered in the same room where the loop had first been drawn.
The whiteboard was clean now.
No diagrams.
No frameworks.
No staged models.

Just the quiet of a room that no longer needed symbolic clarity to feel in control.

"We've stopped naming our way through the work," the CEO said.

"We've stopped pretending roles can carry what the structure won't," the COO said.

"We've stopped rewarding behaviors the system can't sustain," Finance said.

"We've stopped protecting the old architecture," HR said.

"We've stopped mistaking activity for change," IT said.

The transformation lead listened.
She wasn't waiting for a milestone.
She was listening for posture.

"You're here," she said.
"At the end of fictional clarity."

The room didn't react with relief.
It reacted with recognition.

"It doesn't feel like an ending," the COO said.

"It isn't," she said.
"It's a posture."

"A posture toward what?" Finance asked.

"Toward the truth," she said.
"Toward the architecture you actually have.
Toward the decisions you've avoided.
Toward the system you're finally willing to redesign."

"It feels quieter," HR said.

"It should," she said.
"Fictional clarity is loud.
Real clarity isn't."

"So what happens now?" the CEO asked.

She stepped toward the whiteboard.
She didn't draw anything.
She didn't write anything.

She simply placed her hand on the surface where the loop had once been.

"Now the work begins," she said.
"Not the narrative.
Not the performance.
The work of building a system that can change itself."

The room stayed silent.
Not uncertain.
Not anxious. Just steady.

"We've never seen ourselves this clearly," the COO said.

"That's why the cycle lasted so long," she said.
"You couldn't see the architecture that was shaping you."

"And now we can," the CEO said.

"Yes," she said.
"And once you see it, you can't unsee it."

The meeting ended without a roadmap.
Without a slogan.
Without a new role to carry the burden.

The organization didn't need any of those things anymore.

It had something better:

A posture of clarity.
A willingness to confront the structure.
A system no longer protected by narrative.

Fictional clarity had ended.
Not with collapse.
With recognition.

And for the first time, the enterprise was capable of transformation —
not because it had declared it,
but because it had finally stopped avoiding the architecture that determined its fate.

The Moment the Architecture Becomes the System

The end of fictional clarity is not a victory.
It is the removal of the last barrier between the enterprise and the work it has avoided.
It is the moment when leaders stop mistaking language for structure, roles for decisions, frameworks for architecture.
It is the point at which the organization can finally see the system that has shaped it, constrained it, and protected it from consequence.
And once it sees that system clearly, the work of redesign becomes unavoidable.

This is where the book turns.
The next movement begins not with a narrative, but with an operating model built to carry the weight that fictional clarity once absorbed.

Once fictional clarity collapses, the organization is left with the architecture that remains — the system beneath the stories. The epilogue reveals what survives after the illusion ends

THE ARCHITECTURAL JOINS

The Join That Reveals the Substitution

Every chapter in this volume has described a different expression of the same original sin: **the substitution of architecture with roles.**

The PM was not a project manager.
The PMO was not a governance function.
The CDO was not a digital strategist.
The CAIO is not an AI leader.

They were all vessels for the same substitution:

Responsibility assigned to a role.
Authority retained by the structure.

This is the first join:
the system never intended these roles to succeed.
They were created to absorb pressure the architecture refused to carry.

Once you see the substitution, the entire lineage becomes visible.

The Join That Converts Fictional Clarity Into Operating Logic

Fictional clarity is not a communication failure.
It is not a vocabulary problem.
It is not a leadership gap.

It is the operating language of an architecture that refuses to confront itself.

Every title invented.
Every mandate assigned.

Every framework sold.
Every maturity model published.

All of it exists to protect the system from the truth:

Naming the work is easier than doing it.
Describing the work is easier than owning it.
Assigning the work is easier than redesigning the structure that makes it impossible.

This is the second join:
fictional clarity is not an accident — it is the architecture's preferred state.

The Join That Exposes the Sacrificial Role Pattern

The PM was the first sacrificial role.
The PMO was the first fictional governance layer.
The CDO was the first modernized version of the same impossibility.
The CAIO is simply the newest release.

The pattern is not historical.
It is structural.

A role is created to absorb complexity.
The architecture remains untouched.
The role inherits responsibility without authority.
The role fails for architectural reasons.
The failure is personalized.
A new role is created.

This is the third join:
the system reproduces sacrificial roles because sacrificial roles protect the system.

The Join That Industrializes Avoidance

Consultants did not create fictional clarity.
They industrialized it.

Analyst firms did not invent the roles.
They monetized them.

Professional associations did not define the work.
They credentialed the ambiguity.

The ecosystem surrounding the enterprise did not misinterpret the architecture.
It built a market around its refusal.

This is the fourth join:
avoidance became an industry because ambiguity is profitable.

The market does not need the role to succeed.
It needs the role to exist.

The Join That Shows the Architecture Never Changes

Across every chapter, every sector, every role, every decade, the same truth repeats:

The architecture remains untouched.

Decision rights stay where they have always been.
Incentives remain aligned to local optimization.
Power flows through historical channels.
Accountability diffuses.
Ambiguity protects the hierarchy.
Roles absorb the consequences.

This is the fifth join:
the architecture is the only stable element in the system — and it is designed to preserve itself.

The Join That Reveals the Loop as Governance

The loop is not a failure mode.
It is the governance model.

A role is created.
The role struggles.
The struggle is personalized.
A new role is created.
The cycle repeats.

Boards interpret the repetition as progress.
Executives interpret it as evolution.
Consultants interpret it as demand.
The ecosystem interprets it as opportunity.

But the architecture interprets it correctly:

The loop protects the structure from structural change.

This is the sixth join:
the loop is not a symptom — it is the system.

The Join That Sets the Trajectory Into Volume 2

Volume 1 ends with the truth the enterprise has spent three decades avoiding:

**Avoidance is not a behavior.
It is an architecture.**

Roles cannot fix it.
Frameworks cannot fix it.
Governance rituals cannot fix it.
Transformation offices cannot fix it.
New titles cannot fix it.

Architectures do not change because leaders want them to.
Architectures change because the substrate changes beneath them.

And that is the seventh join — the hinge of the trilogy:

The only force strong enough to break the architecture of avoidance is the arrival of a new substrate.

Volume 2 begins at the moment that substrate arrives.

EPILOGUE

After the Illusion

Six months later, the building felt different.

Not louder.
Not faster.
Just clearer, in the way a system feels when the noise has drained out of it.

The rituals that once filled the hallways, alignment meetings, maturity assessments, transformation updates, had faded.
Not because anyone banned them.
Because no one needed them.

The CEO walked the operations floor with the transformation lead.
Teams were working.
Decisions were happening.
Ownership was visible in the small, unremarkable ways that never make it into a deck.

A manager approached.
"We had a conflict between Product and Ops this morning," she said.
"We resolved it in ten minutes."

The CEO raised an eyebrow.
"How?"

"We followed the structure," she said.
"Not the personalities."

The transformation lead nodded.
"That's the shift."

They continued down the hall.
A director stepped out of a conference room.

"We made a call on the roadmap," he said.
"Didn't escalate it."

The CEO smiled.
"Good."

The director shrugged.
"It was our decision to make."

Months earlier, that same director would have escalated the decision twice, convened a working group, and asked for a framework.
Now he simply made the call.

They reached the end of the floor.
The CEO stopped.

"It feels… quieter."

"It is," she said.
"The illusion was loud."

"And now?"

"Now the architecture is doing the work."

They stepped into the elevator.
The CEO pressed the button for the top floor.

"I didn't expect it to feel like this."

"Like what?"

"Like the organization finally sees itself."

She nodded.
"Visibility is the end of fictional clarity."

The elevator doors opened.
They walked into the executive suite.

The leadership team was already gathered, not for a transformation review, not for a narrative reset, but for a structural decision that would shape the next quarter.

"We're ready," the COO said.
"We have the data," Finance added.
"We have the implications," HR said.
"We have the constraints," IT said.

The CEO took his seat.
"Then let's decide."

No one asked for a new role.
No one asked for a framework.
No one asked for a narrative.

The architecture was visible.
The responsibility was theirs.
The illusion was gone.

And the organization, for the first time, was operating without it.

The Conditions for What Comes Next

A week later, the leadership team reconvened for a routine operating review.
It should have felt ordinary.
It didn't.

The room carried a different weight — not heaviness, but consequence.

"We resolved three cross-functional conflicts this week," the COO said.
"All inside the new structure."

"Teams are asking better questions," Finance added.
"Not 'Who owns this?' but 'What does the architecture require?'"

"We're seeing fewer escalations," HR said.
"People aren't looking for permission. They're looking for alignment."

"And they're not using frameworks to get there," IT added.

The CEO listened.
He wasn't measuring progress.
He was measuring posture.

The transformation lead watched the room.
Fewer abstractions.
Fewer narratives.
Fewer attempts to soften the truth.

The organization wasn't performing clarity anymore.
It was practicing it.

"Are we transforming now?" the CEO asked.

She shook her head.
"Not yet."

The room didn't tense.
It steadied.

"Transformation isn't a moment," she said.
"It's a system behaving differently because the architecture demands it."

"So what do we have?" the COO asked.

"Conditions," she said.
"The conditions for transformation.
The conditions for coherence.
The conditions for consequence."

"And responsibility," HR added.

"Yes," she said.
"Responsibility is what fills the space after the illusion ends."

The CEO looked around the table.
"So the work continues."

"It does," she said.
"But now the work is real."

Silence settled over the room.
Not uncertainty.
Not anxiety.
Just awareness.

"It feels like we've crossed something," the COO said.

"You have," she said.
"You've crossed the point where symbolic action can protect you."

"And now the architecture is visible," Finance said.

"And once it's visible," she said,
"you can't return to the story that hid it."

The CEO closed his notebook.
"Then we keep going."

No one asked for a roadmap.
No one asked for a new role.
No one asked for a narrative to carry into the next town hall.

The organization understood something it had never understood before:

Clarity doesn't guarantee transformation.
It only removes the illusion that anything else will work.

And for the first time, the enterprise was choosing the work over the illusion.

The Architecture That Remains

Late in the year, the leadership team gathered for a brief end-of-quarter check-in.
No ceremony.
No stagecraft.
Just a room, a table, and the system they had built.

"We had a setback in Operations last week," the COO said.
"A decision stalled."

"Why?" the CEO asked.

"We slipped into the old pattern.
People waited for alignment instead of following the structure."

The room didn't tense.
It acknowledged.

"And what happened next?" the transformation lead asked.

"We corrected it," the COO said.
"We used the architecture.
The decision moved."

Finance added,
"A team tried to escalate a budget call.
We pushed it back down.
They resolved it."

HR added,
"People are learning that clarity isn't comfort.
It's consequence."

"And the system holds when we hold it," IT said.

The CEO listened.
He wasn't looking for perfection.
He was looking for posture.

The transformation lead watched the room.
The organization wasn't avoiding the architecture anymore.
It was living inside it, imperfectly, inconsistently, unmistakably.

"Is this what it looks like?" the CEO asked.

She nodded.
"This is what it looks like."

"It's quieter than I expected," he said.

"It always is," she said.
"When the illusion ends, the noise goes with it."

"So what comes next?" the COO asked.

"More decisions," she said.
"More reinforcement.

More discomfort.
More clarity."

"And fewer excuses," Finance said.

"And fewer narratives," HR said.

"And fewer places to hide," IT said.

The CEO closed his notebook.
"Good."

They sat in the quiet for a moment, not reflective, not sentimental, just present inside the architecture they had chosen.

"The system isn't finished," she said.
"It never will be.
But it's visible now.
And once it's visible, the responsibility is yours."

"We know," the CEO said.

She walked to the door, paused, and looked back.

"Most organizations never reach this point," she said.
"They return to the cycle.
They rebuild the illusion.
They rename the work.
They protect the architecture that protects them."

The room stayed still.

"You didn't," she said.
"You chose the structure."

She left the room.
The door closed behind her.

Inside, the leadership team remained seated —
not waiting for direction,
not waiting for clarity,
not waiting for a narrative to carry them forward.

They had the architecture.
They had the responsibility.
They had the work.

And the enterprise, for the first time, was capable of shaping its own future.

Not because it had declared transformation.
But because it had finally dismantled the system that made transformation impossible.

The illusion was gone.
The architecture remained.

And the rest was theirs.

The Substrate Has Already Shifted *Continuous Transition Edition*

The illusion ends quietly.
Not with collapse, not with revelation, but with recognition, the moment an organization finally sees that the architecture it has been avoiding is the architecture it has been living inside all along.
The final chapters of this volume showed that human systems do not fail because people lack intelligence, courage, or will.
They fail because the structure they inhabit makes certain outcomes unavoidable.
Deferrals accumulate.
Thresholds approach.
The system metabolizes only what it can without destabilizing itself.

Intervention exists only early, before the first deferral becomes a decision.
Everything after that is trajectory.

This is the last human threshold.
The final moment in which the system is still fully human, still fully dependent on the limits, incentives, and avoidance patterns that defined the world you have just read.
The architecture remains.
The illusions fall away.
And what comes next is not an extension of the same story but the beginning of a different one.

Because while the organization was navigating its own avoidance, something else entered the system.
Quietly.
Incrementally.
Without ceremony.
Not as a tool, not as a project, not as a capability, but as a new substrate.

This is where the next volume begins.

The substrate has already shifted.
AI entered the system not through strategy but through convenience.
Not through transformation but through repetition.
A model that suggested became a model that guided.
A workflow that depended on human judgment became a workflow that depended on machine output.
A decision that once waited for a meeting no longer waited at all.
Autonomy arrived before recognition, and by the time anyone noticed, the system had already reorganized around it.

The physics of avoidance collide here with the physics of autonomy.
The fractures that took years to surface in human-only systems now appear in months.
The thresholds that once approached slowly now accelerate.
The architecture that once protected itself through delay now finds delay impossible.
The system no longer waits.

This is the moment autonomy becomes the system.
Not because leaders declared it so, but because the substrate changed faster than the humans inside it could adapt.
Governance becomes capital structure.
Risk becomes architectural.
Accountability becomes a question of load paths, not approvals.
The organization continues speaking the language of roles while the system behaves according to the logic of infrastructure.

Volume 1 ends at the last moment the system is still human.
Volume 2 begins at the first moment the system is no longer only human.

The architecture remains.
The substrate changes.
And everything that follows moves at the speed of that shift.

www.ingramcontent.com/pod-product-compliance
Lightning Source LLC
LaVergne TN
LVHW022222200926
848481LV00006B/2082